D1441845

MAY   2003

Reefs
and
Rain Forests

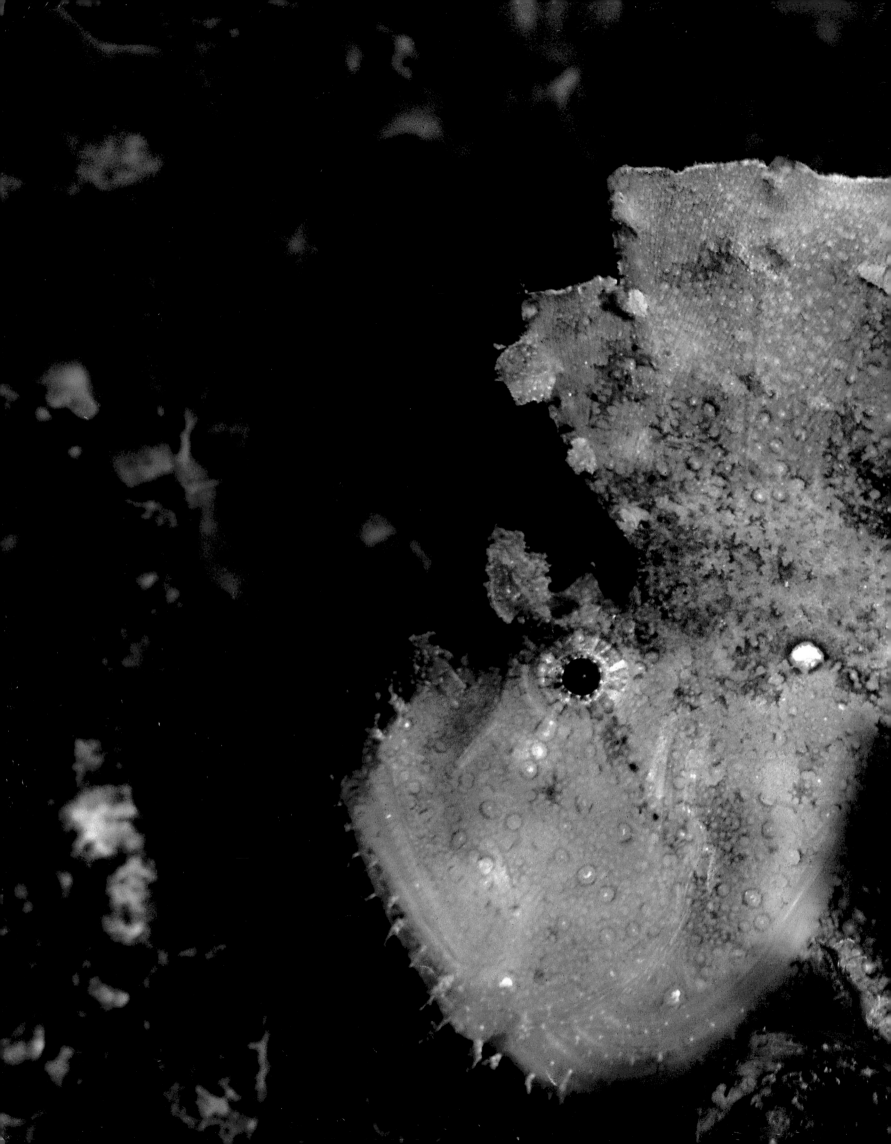

Reefs
and
Rain Forests

The Natural Heritage
of Malaysian Borneo

Murray S. Kaufman

REEFS AND RAIN FORESTS PUBLICATIONS

Reefs and Rain Forests Publications

Beverly Hills, California 90210

© 2002 by Murray S. Kaufman

All rights reserved. Published in 2002

Printed in Singapore by Tien Wah Press Ltd.

Photographs and text © 2002 by Murray S. Kaufman

Photo credits: pp. 189 (bottom), 192–93—Tengku Datuk Dr. Zainal Adlin; p. 141—in collaboration with Richard McEnery; p. 207—Lea Eckerling Kaufman. All rights reserved.

ISBN 0-97106-55-0-0

Fine prints, books, and information about Murray S. Kaufman's work are available through:

Reefs and Rain Forests Publications

608 North Sierra Drive

Beverly Hills, California 90210

Fax: 310.278.8844

Email: murray@murraykaufman.com

http://www.murraykaufman.com

For Aaron and Jenny

Proboscis monkeys

WWF

A PORTION OF THE PROCEEDS FROM THE SALE OF THIS BOOK WILL BE DONATED TO WWF MALAYSIA

Contents

Clouded leopard

Foreword

In our world, the environment is of the utmost importance for our survival. Reefs and rain forests represent the richest ecosystems on Earth, both of which we appreciate as unique systems of life, harboring the greatest diversity of living organisms on our planet.

To be able to share this richness is a collective responsibility: Science has to document and understand the nature of this life, writers and photographers need to portray the wonders and uniqueness, and resource managers (from government to all manner of entrepreneurship) must organize and support administrative systems for protection, conservation, and education. The essence of this great wealth of biodiversity is that it represents part of our living world, ours to protect and to manage wisely. The first step, always, is discovery. This discovery should transcend organizational boundaries because everyone should be able to appreciate the multifaceted wonders of nature.

They say in some instances, to get to know something is a prerequisite to being able to love it. Discovery is thus the key to appreciation and this cannot be more true in the case of nature. Works such as the present one, therefore, are a crucial medium by which to convey this understanding of nature. The pictures and the information in the text carry with them dedicated experience not only in discovery and understanding these rich ecosystems, but also in presenting them in a holistic way.

In this regard, Malaysian Borneo, made up of the states of Sabah and Sarawak, is known as an especially rich territory in terms of species and natural landscapes. Early visitors to the region have always held Borneo as an icon of mystery, of things to be discovered, and of the culmination of the natural inclination for adventure. This still applies today. Borneo remains an exciting destination because as science and discovery progress, we begin to appreciate the enormity of this incredible wealth of nature.

Discovery begins when we take that first step, which has to be from inside ourselves. This book is a certain catalyst for that process, for discovering and appreciating nature is among the finest aspects of human learning.

Datuk Seri Dr. Mahathir bin Mohamad
Prime Minister of Malaysia

To the Readers

Today, at the beginning of the new millennium, we are seeing overwhelming advances in science, technology, and industry on a daily basis. Even with the huge challenges that this new knowledge brings to our daily lives, we must not forget the lessons than can be learned from an appreciation of the natural world around us. Our ecosystems must not be forgotten in our efforts to modernize and keep pace with technology.

Sabah, Malaysia is blessed with a natural heritage of tremendous biodiversity, unrivaled anywhere on our planet. This abundance of indigenous flora and fauna is best represented by our tropical rain forests and coral reefs, possibly the oldest of their types on earth. This volume by Murray S. Kaufman, *Reefs and Rain Forests, the Natural Heritage of Malaysian Borneo*, through the use of spectacular photographs and fascinating text, transports the reader to these places of awe and wonder and increases our understanding and appreciation of these magnificent places.

The rain forests and coral reefs of Malaysian Borneo are treasures that are of importance to all of us. This book will increase our awareness and understanding of these delicate and fragile ecosystems, so that we may play our part in protecting and preserving this natural heritage for future generations to come.

Datuk Chong Kah Kiat
Chief Minister
Sabah, Malaysia

Bigmouth triplefin

Sabah, one of the thirteen states of Malaysia, has phenomenal biodiversity in her coral reefs and tropical rain forests—ecosystems with biological richness unmatched anywhere else on Earth. Nowhere can a visitor see a broader scope of flora and fauna than that which is contained within these easily accessible places. Sabah is truly a remarkable jewel in Malaysia's crown.

Despite these fascinating natural heritage attractions, ecotourists are only now becoming aware of the wealth that Sabah has to offer. Where else can a visitor come face to face with orangutans in the oldest rain forests on our planet, or swim with turtles as they return to their ancestral breeding places? Where else can visitors explore reefs teeming with marine life or climb to the summit of the highest mountain in Southeast Asia, Mount Kinabalu, home to the greatest variety of plants in the world? All of this and more can be easily experienced in this land of warm, welcoming, English-speaking people. Furthermore, an infrastructure with luxury accommodations and modern transportation is already in place for visitors.

Reefs and Rain Forests, the Natural Heritage of Malaysian Borneo, by Murray S. Kaufman, is to be commended for its outstanding contribution in promoting awareness and appreciation of Sabah, Malaysian Borneo. This important book invites you to begin your personal discovery of the natural heritage of the "Land Below the Wind."

Dato' Abdul Kadir B. HJ. Sheikh Fadzir
Minister of Culture, Arts and Tourism Malaysia

Golden damselfish in soft coral

Long-tailed macaque

Preface

This book is the product of my travels to Malaysia's coral reefs and rain forests spanning more than seven years, an attempt to bring alive the immensity and spark, and even the strangeness, of what are considered by many to be the oldest ecosystems on Earth. It is an attempt to open a door to a part of the world little known and rarely visited by Westerners: the last living Eden, perhaps, from which everything is a descendant, an offshoot, or a distant relation. The many wondrous creatures you'll meet here have affected me deeply by their beauty and mystery and, over time, by their haunting ephemerality as we continue to destroy their natural habitats.

As a photographer, I hope the need for conservation will seem more pressing and real to you as you see what is at stake: in the intelligent eyes of the orangutan and the changing hues of the cuttlefish. Today, thousands of acres in Malaysian Borneo have been designated as national parks, wildlife reserves, and wildlife rehabilitation centers, due in part to the efforts of Tengku Datuk Dr. Zainal Adlin, who has generously written the conservation chapter for this book. I'm honored by the participation of Professors Ridzwan Abdul Rahman and K.M. Wong, who have shared their scientific knowledge as a way of introducing the photographs. In my repeated travels throughout Malaysian Borneo, I've come to appreciate the need for conserving the reefs and rain forests as never before, and hope that this book can be part of a worldwide effort.

Photographs cannot capture the smells and sounds of the rain forest, the vibrant undulation of life in the reefs—they can only lend us a vision and, hopefully, a feeling about a place. Because any in-depth study of the vast ecosystems of the reefs and rain forests would easily fill many volumes, this book is merely an introduction. Perhaps a few words about the organization of the book would be appropriate here. Following a brief introduction, there are three main chapters: "Reefs," "Rain Forests," and "Regarding Conservation." Each of these chapters begins with an essay by an expert in the field who is also a Malaysian. A stranger to this special part of the world could not describe it with the passion and concern of those whose very lives are bound up in its beauty and fragility. Each written essay is followed by a photo essay that aspires to do justice to the reality of Malaysian Borneo. I kept captions to a minimum in this section to avoid intellectual distractions, but realizing that information about the locations, scientific names, and the exact circumstances of the images might be of interest to some, I included a lengthy annotation, "Photographer's Notes," which attempts to address this need. These notes and thumbnail photos are organized in sequential order and indexed with the page numbers of the photographs as they appear in the main chapters of the book. This way, if supplemental information is desired, it should be simple to locate. "Photographer's Notes" can also be read as a kind of narrative on its own. For the curious photographers among you, I included a page, "Technical Notes," with specifics about the equipment used to make the pictures.

It is my hope that this book will inspire and entice you to visit and learn more about Malaysian Borneo. It is truly one of the most exuberantly alive, and essential, places on Earth.

Murray S. Kaufman

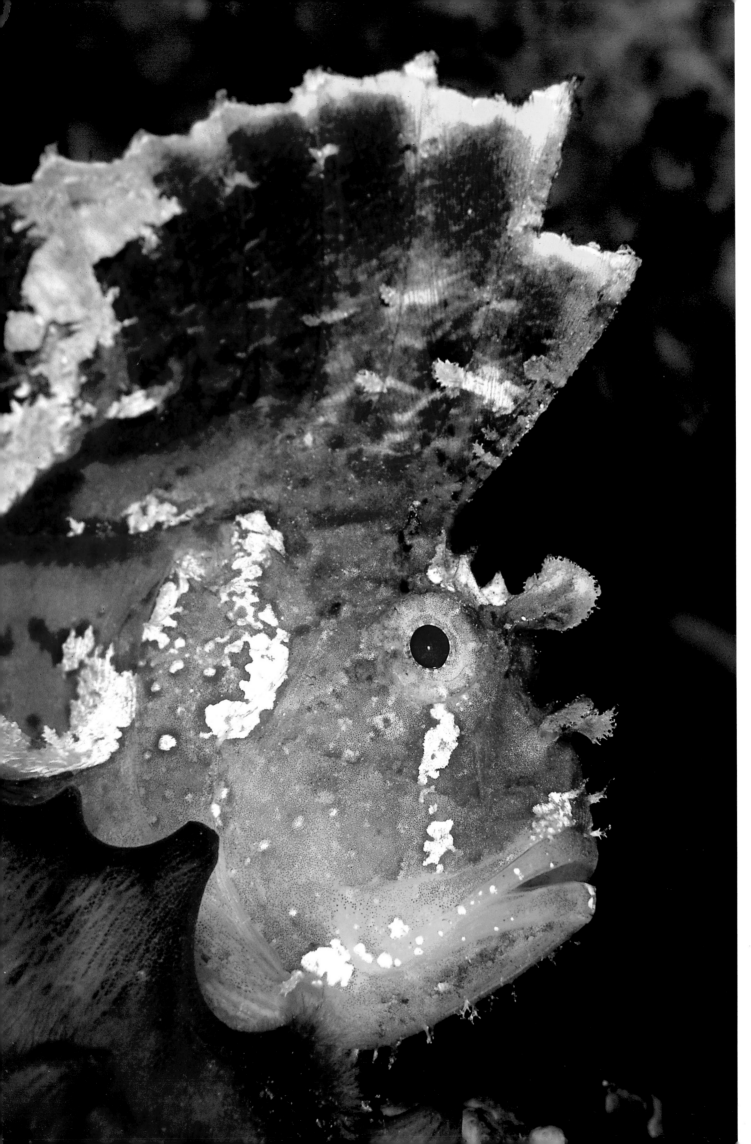

Leaf scorpionfish

Acknowledgments

My passion for nature photography began rather naively in 1988, during my first live-aboard scuba diving trip to the Cayman Islands. I'd only just learned how to dive, and was still uncomfortable doing it. Onboard the boat, I met the "photo-pro" Gerald Freeman, a New Jersey doctor who'd chucked it all to become a dive guide in the Caymans. He'd worked with well-known underwater photography teacher, Jim Church, and was starting an underwater photography course based on Jim's world-renowned method of teaching. He talked me into signing up.

At the first class, he took out a Nikonos amphibious camera and exclaimed, "This is the front and this is the back. Got it?" and I nodded uncertainly. Minutes later, when he talked about shutter speeds and f-stops, he lost me completely. I made the first few dives with camera in hand, turned the film in for processing and the first rolls came back totally black! I decided my career in photography was over, but Gerald insisted on looking at the film. Rather than ridicule me, he took me by the hand and showed me the basics. By the second day, I was actually producing images!

I quickly learned that underwater photography is highly addictive and consuming—of time and money. Who else but a crazy person would immerse expensive, high-tech electronic devices in salt water? I didn't even realize until much later how difficult underwater photography is. First off, water does some very strange things to light; nearly all images made underwater are partially or totally strobe illuminated. Next, you work in a liquid medium where everything is moving, including yourself. Then there's diving, of course, which has its own inherent risks, including the bends, which means you have limited time underwater. You can't change film or lenses, so you can't shoot more than one roll of film with that camera on a given dive. And there's no way around it: To make truly great images, you need professional equipment (no middle ground between beginner and advanced), and it's expensive. But, when you get a great image back . . . .

I joined the Los Angeles Chapter of the Underwater Photographic Society and entered competitions, which I began winning locally and, later, at the national and international levels. I wrote photo essays for diving magazines and contributed photographs to pieces written by others. Time passed and my passion increased. I met many interesting and accomplished underwater photographers, and began to study their work. My strongest influences have been David Doubilet and Chris Newbert. When I started out underwater, I'd often visualize Doubilet's amazing image of a given subject (often, as seen in the National Geographic) and try to copy him. Many of us started that way, trying to meet or exceed the Doubilet "gold standard" for underwater photography. Whatever image I make, even today, I always remember that he probably did it first. Chris Newbert has been another great influence. His 1985 book, *Within a Rainbowed Sea*, remains a best-selling testament to his skill at capturing the breadth and beauty of underwater life; it is Chris, more than anyone else I know, who has transformed underwater photography into an art. To this day, I'm grateful for his insight, expertise, and friendship. Finally, "on land," my favorite nature photographer (and there are many I admire and respect) is Frans Lanting. His ability to capture the essence or personality of his subjects results in work that is moving, awe-inspiring, and magnificent to behold. He has had a profound impact on my work.

About the time I started photographing in Malaysian

Borneo, I started reading about and experimenting with nature photography on land. I attended a seminar by John and Barbara Gerlach, two wonderful nature photographers and even better teachers, and have since spent time with them in the field. They are an endless source of information, and they never tire of my questions. I owe them a lot.

None of my underwater photographs would ever have been taken if I hadn't learned to scuba dive in the first place. For that, I have to thank Ken Yates, a childhood friend who first introduced me to diving; I needed lots of handholding at first, which Ken never ceased to provide. My "brother" Gerald Freeman deserves my thanks, since he was my first teacher in underwater photography. He has been one of my strongest advocates. My thanks and appreciation to Richard McEnery, a versatile travel, nature and sports photographer. He was my dive buddy and companion on my first three trips to Borneo. His enthusiasm, support, advice and feedback were essential to me as I formulated the idea and began implementing it to create this book. And thanks to my good friend and fellow photographer, Tony Frank, for his support and ongoing good counsel as I've struggled through this process. He has been one of my best dive buddies and one of my strongest critics.

Juvenile fingered dragonet

In Malaysian Borneo, there are a number of people I want to recognize. My first guide through the rain forest, Benjamin Managil, has been a great friend and companion. A jungle guide since he was very young, Ben's vast knowledge and experience have proved indispensable in creating many of my rain forest images. Extremely proud of his natural heritage, Ben sings beautifully, charms every woman he meets, and is truly liked by everyone. I also want to thank Simon Ambi of the Borneo Rainforest Lodge in the Danum Valley, for his help in getting images of reclusive and rare subjects, such as the tarsier. In many ways, Simon and Ben are lay biologists, so it is in this light that I must also acknowledge my third main guide, Mohd. Zaini A. Wahab, a self-taught scholar and naturalist with a tremendous knowledge of Mount Kinabalu and its environs. I've had some amazing experiences with Zaini; he actually saved my life one harrowing night on a trek down Mount Kinabalu in the dark (a story for another time!).

As in the rain forest, my underwater guides have been wonderfully helpful, as have the diving resorts. My appreciation to Ken Pan, Douglas Leong, and Hiroshi Nomura at the Sipadan Water Village on Mabul Island for their beautiful accommodations, efficient staff, and outstanding diving program; a very special place to live and work. Yoshi Hirata, a marine biologist and excellent underwater photographer, was instrumental in finding many of the rare, exotic, and unusual subjects I photographed. Thanks to my tireless guides Leonard Lai, Su Kian Tiong, and Miki Tanaka, and special thanks to Alex Ho, the greatest dive guide in the world! Alex, like my guides in the rain forest, is a self-taught naturalist who takes great pride in revealing the "secrets" of his underwater world. Without his help, many images in this book would not have been possible.

From our first meeting, Irene Benggon Charuruks, General Manager of the Sabah Tourism Promotion Corporation, has been a friend, supporter, and confidant. She has given her time and attention tirelessly on behalf of the book, in her goal of promoting greater understanding and appreciation of Sabah throughout the world. It was Irene who introduced me to many of the government officials who, in turn, have supported this project.

I owe a huge debt of gratitude to Datuk Chong Kah Kiat, who was the Sabah Minister of Tourism Development,

Environment, Science, and Technology during much of the time I spent photographing. His support has been immeasurable. Just before this book went to press, Datuk Chong was promoted to Chief Minister, the highest office in Sabah. His love for his homeland and his vision for the future portend great things for Sabah. Also, because of Datuk Chong's generous introduction, I was welcomed into the home of the Prime Minister of Malaysia, Datuk Seri Dr. Mahathir bin Mohamad, who was kind, gracious, inquisitive, and praiseworthy about the project. I am truly honored to have the Prime Minister's foreword grace this book.

One of the major driving forces behind this project from the beginning, Tengku Datuk Dr. Zainal Adlin is possibly the most incredible man I have ever met. The name "Tengku" means prince; he is a descendent of the Sultan of Kelantan, a state of Western (Peninsular) Malaysia. Although not Sabahan by birth, he has spent much of his life here and he has a tremendous love for Sabah. His list of accomplishments is enormous. As a young man, he was trained by the British to be a fighter pilot. Later, he entered civil service as a city planner/housing developer. Ultimately, he became Deputy Director of the multifaceted Yayasan Sabah (Sabah Foundation), where he oversaw the timber industry and forest management (among other responsibilities). The driving force behind much of the development of Kota Kinabalu (Sabah's capital), Tengku is also an explorer. He's led numerous expeditions throughout Sabah, including his first love, Mount Kinabalu, and has helped to open new routes and areas of exploration. Passionate about conservation, he was responsible for the gazetting of the Danum Valley Conservation Area, a 2.5-million-acre area of virgin lowland rain forest that is now protected from logging and houses a reforestation research center. In 1988, a newly discovered species of the rare *Rafflesia* flower, *Rafflesia tengku-adlinii*, was named in his honor. As a long-term Trustee and now Chairman of the World Wildlife Fund (WWF) Malaysia, he received the Duke of Edinburgh Conservation Medal from Prince Philip for his environmental work. A true Renaissance man, Tengku has dedicated his life to preserving the environment. He is a soft-spoken, gentle, and extremely humble individual, and he has inspired me greatly.

Back in the States, I want to thank my partner in surgical practice, Dr. Douglas Galen, for "holding down the fort" while I've been away in the jungle or reefs, and also manager Joyce Botelho and my entire office staff, for their patience, understanding, and continuing support.

I want to thank Nancy Lambert for her outstanding initial editing of the text. I am grateful to my wife, art historian Lea Eckerling Kaufman, who shared her expertise and devoted much time in the selection and presentation of the images that form the core of this work. Many thanks to Charles Mohr, of L. A. Book Arts, an authority in the world of fine art book publishing, who offered his immense knowledge without reservation, and to Hossein Farmani, Tanja Paajanen, Doug Smith, Homa Ferdowsi, and Rudi Weislein of Fontographics in Los Angeles, for their fantastic work in producing the graphic design and digital files so crucial to completing this book. Also, I want to thank Irina Averkieff for information architecture and design, and Stefan Klima for final proof-reading.

Lowland rain forest

Finally, I want to thank my wife, Lea, and my children, Aaron and Jenny. I'm sure that at times they thought I was crazy, obsessed, and "over the edge" with this project, but they were always very tolerant and supportive. Without their love and understanding, my dream would not have become a reality.

Major Sponsors

SABAH
TOURISM

INNOPRISE

malaysia
AIRLINES

NEPAL

BHUTAN

CHINA

Shangh

Thimphu

Kathmandu

INDIA

Dhaka

MYANMAR
(BURMA)

Nanning

Hong
Kong

Ta

Kolkata
(Calcutta)

BANGLADESH

Hanoi

LAOS

TAIWAN

Bay
of
Bengal

Vientiane

Rangoon

THAILAND

South
China

Bangkok

VIETNAM

Sea

Manila

CAMBODIA

Phnom Penh

Ho Chi Minh City

10°N

SPRATLY ISLANDS

Kota Kinabalu

BRUNEI

MALAYSIA

MALAYSIA

Medan

Kuala Lumpur

Kuching

SINGAPORE

BORNEO

0°

INDIAN

SUMATRA

INDON

Pontianak

Samarinda

Palembang

Banjarmasin

SULAWE

Makassar

Jakarta

OCEAN

JAVA

Surabaya

Sumbawa

Bali

10°S

Sumba

N

0   500 mi

0   500 km

© Equator Graphics, Inc.

90°E

100°E

110°E

120

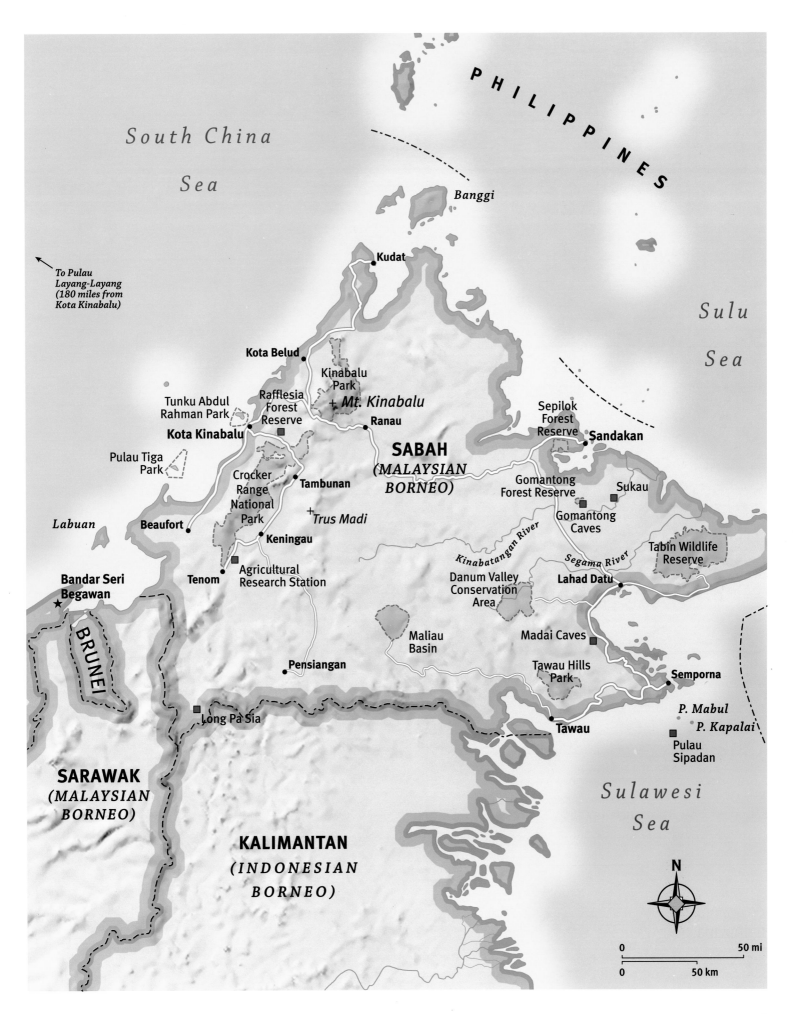

PHILIPPINES

South China

Sea

Banggi

Sulu

Sea

To Pulau
Layang-Layang
(180 miles from
Kota Kinabalu)

Kudat

Kota Belud

Kinabalu
Park

Tunku Abdul
Rahman Park

Rafflesia
Forest
Reserve

+ *Mt. Kinabalu*

Sepilok
Forest
Reserve

Kota Kinabalu

Ranau

Sandakan

Pulau Tiga
Park

SABAH
*(MALAYSIAN
BORNEO)*

Crocker
Range
National
Park

Tambunan

Gomantong
Forest Reserve

Sukau

Labuan

Beaufort

+ *Trus Madi*

Keningau

Kinabatangan River

Segama River

Tabin Wildlife
Reserve

**Bandar Seri
Begawan**

★

Agricultural
Research Station

Tenom

Gomantong
Caves

Danum Valley
Conservation
Area

Lahad Datu

BRUNEI

Maliau
Basin

Madai Caves

Pensiangan

Tawau Hills
Park

Semporna

Long Pa Sia

P. Mabul

P. Kapalai

Tawau

Pulau
Sipadan

SARAWAK
*(MALAYSIAN
BORNEO)*

*Sulawesi
Sea*

KALIMANTAN

*(INDONESIAN
BORNEO)*

N

0   50 mi

0   50 km

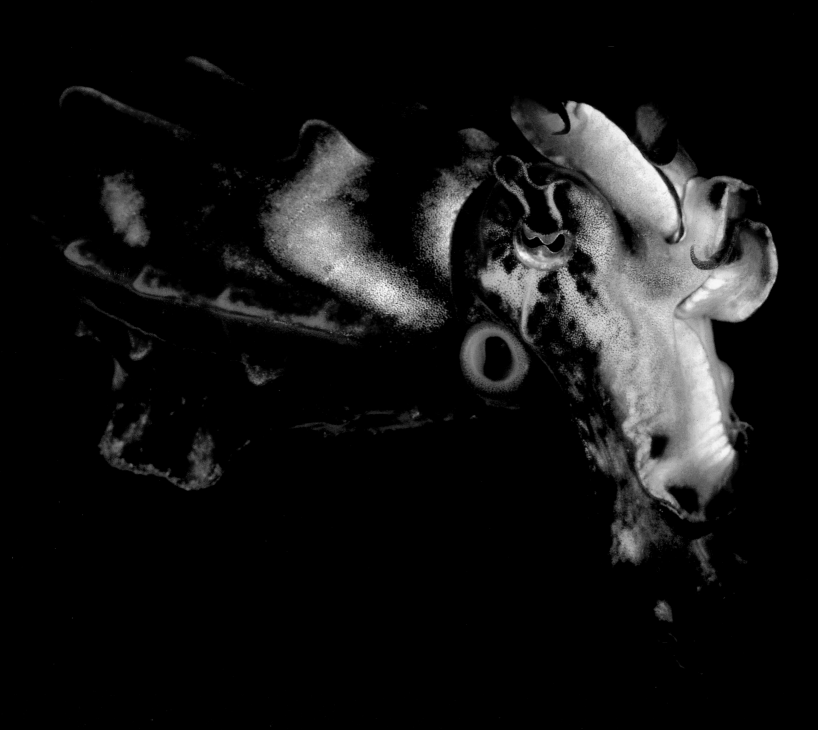

Flamboyant cuttlefish

Introduction

Of all the untamed places on Earth, none are as enigmatic and compelling as the coral reef and the tropical rain forest. Distant from civilization, ancient and self-contained, these ecosystems open a door into our past while providing the natural abundance to sustain us in the present and replenish our future. For years, people have traveled to reefs and rain forests seeking adventure and simplicity, wisdom and delight. We've come to understand that rain forests and reefs hold clues to the mysteries of human nature and ecological balance, but we've tended to view them separately, as discrete ecosystems. Rarely has the opportunity been taken to explore reefs and rain forests side by side, in a place where they almost literally touch.

Borneo, the third largest island in the world, comprises three countries: Malaysia, in the north, divided into the states of Sabah and Sarawak; the tiny nation of Brunei, located between Sabah and Sarawak; and the Indonesian state of Kalimantan, which occupies the remainder.

For generations, people have been lured to this region by tales of flying snakes and Dragon's-blood; mystic curative powers associated with the tusk of the rhinoceros; and strange, prehistoric flowers. The state of Sabah, called the "Land Below the Wind," drew visitors because of its location south of the typhoon belt and its safe harbor. Nineteenth-century British traders came seeking rattan for furniture and camphor for medicine. And explorers continue to arrive today in hopes of meeting the "Old Man of the Forest"—the solitary orangutan, living high in the arboreal canopy. Despite the stories of adventure passed between travelers from every part of the world, and present-day invasions by tourists and scientists, the island of Borneo remains a mystery.

I went there for the first time in the spring of 1994, tantalized by a video I'd seen of a flamboyant cuttlefish, a creature I'd never before seen or heard of in my life. Yet, even as I prepared for my trip, I heard about other rare reef animals—gobies and stargazers, snake eels and corals—which live nowhere else in the world. It would be the diving trip of a lifetime.

When I arrived in the Malaysian state of Sabah, I hardly noticed the rain forests; I was eager to get to Mabul and Sipadan, islands in the Sulawesi Sea less than an hour by boat from Semporna, a small fishing town on Sabah's eastern coast. Sipadan had been popularized about twenty years prior, following a six week-long exploration by Jacques Cousteau on the *Calypso*, after which he pronounced Sipadan "an untouched piece of art," more pristine than any site he'd visited in more than forty-five years. An oceanic island, formed by reef-building coral that colonized cooling lava following a cataclysmic underwater eruption, Sipadan is known today for its huge colony of sea turtles, schools of barracudas and jacks, and the sudden, dramatic plunge of its walls to a depth of 2,800 feet just fifteen feet offshore. It's a tiny place; one can walk around the island in less than forty minutes. Surrounded by reefs harboring life of such great biodiversity, many scientists feel this region saw the genesis of the earth's oceans. Just twenty minutes away, the lesser-known island of Mabul is being increasingly recognized for its wide array of smaller marine life, what photographers call critters or macrosubjects. Surrounded by fringing reefs, Mabul's coconut palms stand in vibrant contrast to the miniature rain forest at the center of Sipadan. Even closer to Sipadan than Mabul, Kapalai Island is actually a large sand bar with a very extensive system of patch and fringing reefs where many new and unusual fishes and invertebrates have been discovered. Located in the channel between Semporna and Mabul, divers have recently begun exploration of an extensive, open-water, reef system known as the Ligitan Reef. This pristine reef arises from the ocean floor at depths of sixty to seventy feet and approaches within fifteen feet of the surface. I found all of the islands and their reefs to be gorgeous. The waters were tranquil, warm, and astonishingly clear. The place seemed like Paradise.

Mantis shrimp

In the reefs, I saw gobies and shrimp, eels and anglerfish, clownfish and anemones, butterflyfish and squid—an amazing diversity, more densely packed and numerous than I could ever imagine. Close to a dock on Mabul Island, mere steps from the base of a ladder, in shallow water, I was overjoyed to discover a wide array of macrosubjects and juveniles, more than I'd ever seen before in such a small area in my life. Returning to dive in the knee-deep mangrove swamps on the Sabah coast, I found an equally broad range of strange macrosubjects skirting the muddy, muck-generating bottom, where terrestrial and marine life meet. I photographed shoaling barracudas and jacks, all the way down to shrimp and crabs as tiny as my fingernail, missing shots because my lens was too large, or too small, and the moment would slip irretrievably away. I marveled at the textures, patterns and colors of the coral gardens, and soon located the elusive cuttlefish that had enticed me to Malaysia in the first place; flashing luminous yellow- and rose-colored tentacles as it fed on its prey, lumbering forward, tentacles swaying like the trunk of an elephant. Entranced, I photographed mantis shrimp and leaf fish, groupers and triggerfish, dotty backs, snappers, and sweetlips. I shot a blue ringed octopus and manta rays, shrimp swathed in anemone houses, butterflyfish and mandarinfish, a sea horse, a stargazer peering up through the sandy bottom as if he were part of it. I basked in the weightless serenity of the reef and photographed a thorny oyster in its cave, bizarre and beautiful, encrusted in red and pink sponges, its twin rows of eyes seeming to peer at me through a mantle of orange, white, and blue.

I didn't truly pay attention to the rain forest until my third trip, even though I passed it many times on my way to the Sulawesi Sea islands—a luxurious curtain shimmering in the humidity. With each trip past the rain forest, that elusive, impenetrable wall of green exuded such a cacophony of sounds—the distant shrieks of birds and cries of apes, an omnipresent buzz of insects and whirring of wings so that the canopy itself seemed a living thing, beckoning me inside. My guides, answering my endless questions, talked about legendary prehistoric flowers, columns of lianas winding up the trunks of trees so high they touched the clouds. I quickly discovered that the animals in the rain forest were as swift and elusive as anything found in the reefs.

Seeing proboscis monkeys cavorting in the trees lining the Kinabatangan River led me to assume that making good pictures would be easy. Their antics seemed made for the camera, as did the endless sweep and interplay of the hornbills, broadbills, and kingfishers; the macaques and leaf monkeys; the snakes, crocodiles, lizards, and insects. The riverbanks were lined with yellow flowers called *Dillenia*, delicate and beautiful. A hornbill landed on a picnic table, and a buffy fish-owl perched in a tree outside my window. In the stillness before dawn, the river seemed truly primeval, blanketed in mist, the cycle of rebirth and decay producing a smell almost achingly verdant.

I ventured into the rain forest at night after my easygoing, amicable guide, Ben Managil, said I couldn't truly know it until I'd walked inside it after dark. We entered together and, within steps, I felt water dripping on my face and looked up, but the stars were completely obscured by the forest canopy. Stumbling on a thick, unpredictable carpet of twigs, fallen lianas, and crumbling vegetation, we'd entered a black universe of sound and smell, including the acrid, urine odor of a tarsier hidden somewhere in the nearby trees. Soon, we saw lizards, snakes, incredible insects. I lit them with my flashlight and took photographs.

The Malaysian rain forests are the oldest tropical rain forests on the planet, with higher trees and with more species of flora and fauna per square quarter mile than exist in all the forests of North America combined. Called the "green lungs" of the earth, average rainfall sometimes exceeds 200 inches a year, and the biodiversity of the rain forest is matched only by that of the coral reefs. The vertical structure of the rain forest and its dense greenery ensure that sunlight entering through the upper canopy is dissipated before reaching the forest floor, which remains in perpetual twilight. Unlike the rain forests in Africa and in the Amazon region, the upper canopy of the Malaysian rain forest varies in height, its emergent trees crowned less evenly than trees in rain forests elsewhere in the world. This minor anomaly, however, has had an enormous impact on the physical evolution of animals living beneath the uneven crown. This striking feature of the Malaysian rain forest has nurtured the differentiation of an astounding variety of tree-dwelling animals with the capability of gliding flight, via webbed feet or actual wings. In Malaysia alone, you can see flying snakes and squirrels, flying frogs, and even web-footed "flying" lemurs launch themselves and glide from branch to branch with unparalleled ease, drifting from the trees of one canopy down to another like strange, beautiful kites. You won't see anything like it anywhere in the world.

Lowland rain forest

A second feature unique to the Malaysian rain forest, specifically in northern Sabah, is the presence of a mountain range to the far north, and Mount Kinabalu, at 13,455 feet, is the tallest peak, by far, in all of Southeast Asia. On its lower slopes begin the tremendous variety of orchids, as well as the *Nepenthes*, or insectivorous pitcher plants, for which the Malaysian rain forests are famed. Further down, descending through the rolling green crown of the forest canopy, an ever-thickening tangle of lianas, mosses, epiphytes, and strangling figs begins to extend vertically, horizontally, and diagonally from every once-visible surface of living bark. As the tangle of vines descends, the number and noise of animals and plants becomes more and more riotous, revealing individual species endemic to specific strata in the forest. For example, the orangutan typically remains in the trees comprising the rain forest's main canopy, the mid-level, living a life of utter solitude, adding to the mystery of our nearest primate cousin, whose visage and habits seem otherwise so akin to our own. An interesting fact about the Malaysian rain forest is the solitary nature of most of its animal inhabitants, which is rather unusual elsewhere. From the tree-dwelling primates and birds, including macaques and hornbills, to a world filled with stick insects, butterflies, lizards, and frogs, the forest continues to descend into deepening shadows. It finally reaches a soil floor that is poor in nutrients and relies on the waste products and carcasses of plants and animals living above to recreate and replenish the nutrients that the forest needs in order to survive. Nowhere is waste recycled more swiftly than in the soil of a rain forest. The termites, fungi, and plants on the floor all play a vital role in this regenerative process. And beneath the soil itself, threads of interconnecting soil fungi and plant roots form the symbiotic latticework known as mycorrhizas, providing nourishment that spreads upward and outward to touch the rain forest canopy.

Maidenveil fungus

The age and unique configuration of the Malaysian rain forest is perhaps no better evidenced than by the presence of the *Rafflesia*, the largest and strangest flower on Earth. Without leaves, stems, or roots, *Rafflesia* cannot synthesize or absorb the nutrients it requires. Instead, it is obliged to infect the roots of the *Tetrastigma*, a woody climbing vine. The flower takes eight to nine months to develop from a tiny bud to its final size, which can be up to three feet in diameter for one of the three Sabah species. At any time, the bud can be eaten by animals or rot. When it blooms, it lasts just three or four days, then dies. Since the biology of this rare flower is poorly understood, it cannot be cultivated. The *Rafflesia* has come to symbolize the delicacy and vulnerability of the Malaysian rain forest and the serious need for conservation of this endangered habitat.

Through repeated visits over seven years, I came to see that the magnificent complexity of the Malaysian rain forest is matched, treasure for treasure, by the outward expansion of marine life in its nearby reefs. The same photosynthesis that brings nourishment to the rain forest gives life to the reefs as well, which is where the food chain technically begins. Here, the formation of coral reefs relies on a single mutually beneficial relationship, that of the coral polyp to an algae called zooxanthellae, which is "farmed" in the coral polyp's tissues. Using the coral polyp's waste products as "fertilizer" in the presence of sunlight, the algae photosynthesize nutrients that are converted by the coral polyp into reef-building calcium carbonate. Over time, spreading out then compressing into limestone, the same coral/algae relationship that gives life to the reef may eventually break the ocean's surface to form the beginnings of an oceanic island, such as Sipadan, or take various other forms. Whatever contiguous shape it eventually takes, the reef's sprawling skeletal cathedrals serve as a testament to the intimate relationship between sunlight and sea, between sea and the formation of land.

An environmentalist I once met, quoting an unknown source, expressed the concept of biodiversity perfectly: "The instructions for running our planet are in the DNA of every living creature. Unfortunately, we are destroying the instructions before we have read them." With each trip to Sabah, I've reached a greater understanding of what biodiversity actually means—that life in the reefs and rain forests is as fragile as it is complex, and that irrevocable harm will be done if we fail to preserve it.

To Westerners and Easterners alike, Malaysia may seem a puzzling place, its people as much a study in contrasts as its reefs and its rain forests. Like the dynamic environment they live in, the people of Malaysia are changing, moving into the future, carrying forth their history as well as their hopes. They bring forth their natural ease to meet challenges, as well as the wisdom to continue preserving their natural heritage in the face of global change that will affect people of all nations. The infrastructure in Malaysia is already in place. Thousands of acres have been designated as national parks, wildlife reserves, and wildlife rehabilitation centers. The creation of an ecotourism bureau, and facilities to house visitors from all over the world, is part of an ongoing effort by the Malaysian government and people to open a dialogue between nations regarding questions of vital importance to the future of our planet.

This book is an invitation. If you feel even a glimmer of the wonder I experienced in the reefs and rain forests of Malaysian Borneo, I'll count it an unqualified success. But you have to go there, of course. See for yourself.

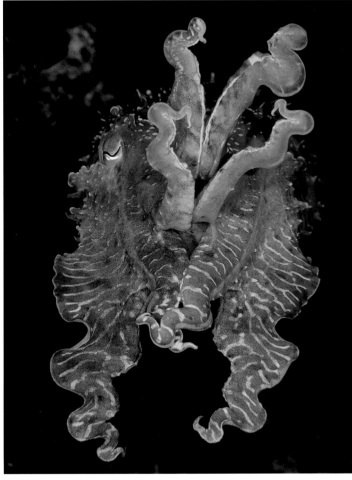

Cuttlefish

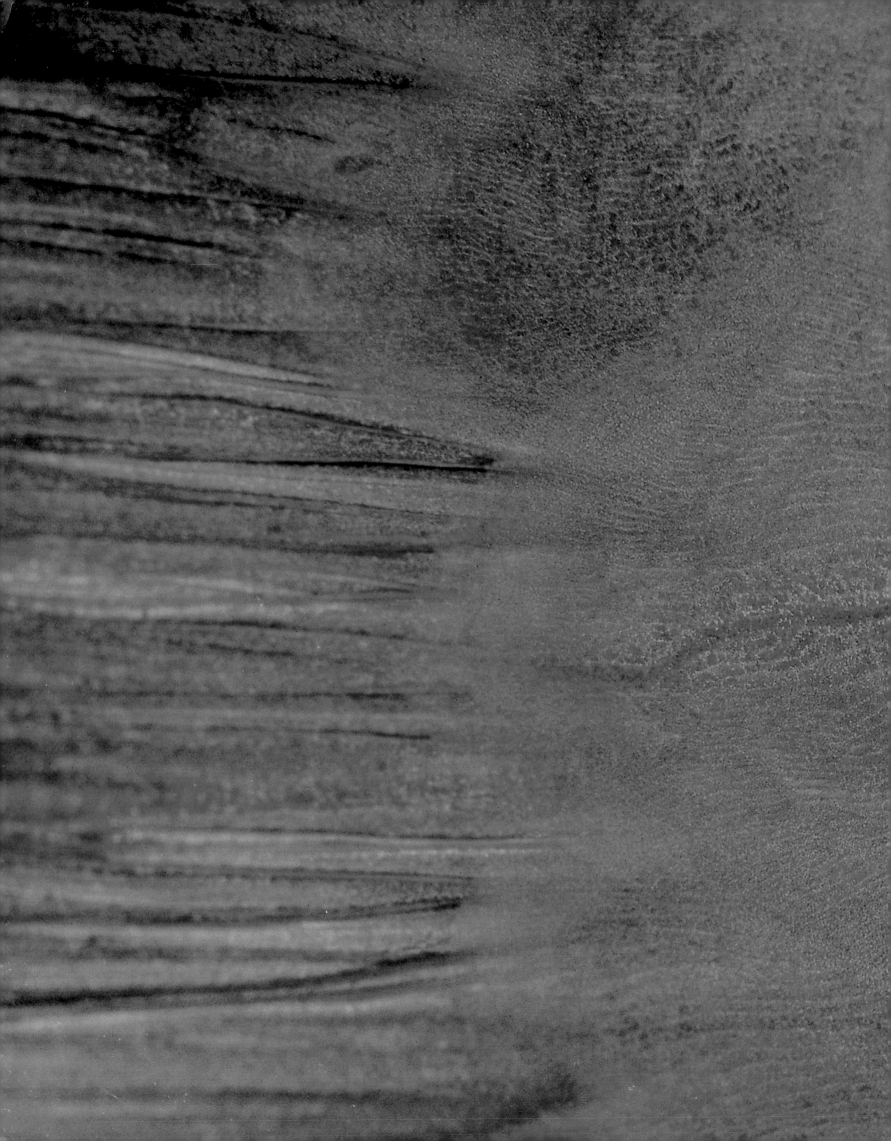

Reefs

Gorgonian sea fans

Reefs

Ridzwan Abdul Rahman, Ph.D.
Associate Professor and Head
Borneo Marine Research Institute
Universiti of Malaya, Sabah

The coral reefs of Malaysian Borneo surpass all other ecosystems in the marine world in beauty and enormity of life. Highly prolific and biologically diverse, the reefs attract not only lovers of nature and natural beauty, but also scientists like myself, who want to learn more about the organizational complexity of the coral reefs native to northeast Borneo, to find answers to questions about the reef's remarkable resilience.

Sabah's impressive coastline, measuring nearly 1,000 miles long, gives it jurisdiction over more than 38,600 square miles of territorial waters in the South China, Sulu, and Sulawesi seas. The marine ecosystems of this region provide conditions that are highly favorable for prodigious coral growth, and hermatypic hard corals, which are distributed throughout the tropics, tend to concentrate here to produce spectacular reefs.

Several types of reefs are encountered in Sabah. Those adjacent to a landmass are called fringing reefs and barrier reefs, with the former occurring near the coast and the latter separated by greater distance and deeper water. These are the most common types of reefs in Sabah. The other type of reef found here is the atoll, a beautiful horseshoe-shaped form emerging out of deep water away from the land. Atolls enclose lagoons, which themselves contain patch reefs.

The widespread distribution of fringing reefs bears testimony to the clear and shallow waters around the mainland and islands. Here, where water currents circulate effectively and the contoured sea bottom protects the back reef from exposure to overheating, an amazing variety of corals thrive in the reef rim, as well as between the rim and the islands. This concurrence of fringing reefs, barrier reefs, and atolls presents a mesmerizing work of nature that is perhaps not seen anywhere else

in the world. To find fringing reefs side by side with mangrove stands, as occurs in many places in Sabah, is also rare.

The amalgamation of landscape and seascape in northeast Borneo also exemplifies an unusual, perhaps unique, interplay of land and sea. Here, where the reef profile is closely integrated with some of the oceanic islands, such as Sipadan, patch reefs are in many places so close to the beach that their rear sides slope into fine sand at a shallow depth on the sunlit continental shelf.

Coral reefs of this region are quite adaptable to sea conditions, accounting for the enormous diversity and natural abundance. Reefs situated away from the mainland, especially those in the South China Sea on Sabah's west coast where the seas are heavy at certain times of year, support coral colonies that are robust and contain strong banks of coralline algae. Waves break over the reef, quickly releasing their energy and leaving the structure intact. Marine life is less dense in such places, although fish like wrasses (which can withstand turbulence) are quite at ease. Everywhere, fish on reef slopes are less abundant and are represented by fewer species than on reef tops. Seagrass beds are often associated with reefs and lagoons, and serve as a cradle for juvenile fish and shellfish.

The Making of the Reef

Reef-building corals derive nutrition from multiple sources. Plankton and organic nutrients, present in great density in the waters off Sabah, are captured and absorbed by the tentacles of coral animals known as polyps, which themselves derive their energy directly from an indispensable, symbiotic relationship with unicellular, yellow-brown algae called zooxanthellae. These algae are contained within the living tissues of the coral polyps. The zooxanthellae produce oxygen and nutrients for coral polyps and, in turn, receive carbon dioxide and the polyp's other waste materials. Also present in great abundance in Sabah's waters are cyanobacteria, unicellular blue-green algae that supply nitrogen to the waters surrounding the reef, and calcareous red algae, which help to bind the coral structures together.

Skeletons of coral polyps are made up of a soluble form of calcium carbonate. During the process of coral nutrition, polyps secrete this material as a way of disposing of excess calcium. As grazing fish and natural causes (such as storms) damage the developing coral skeletons, areas of damage become quickly encrusted with algae, sponges, soft corals, and other invertebrates. Over time, the calcified remains of the reef become compacted and coral rock or limestone is created. Hard or stony corals, made up of thousands of individual coral polyps, are the main reef builders.

Coral polyp

Most reef-building corals are nocturnal. During the day, coral polyps retract down into the skeletal cups that are created as they deposit calcium carbonate around their lower parts. At night, the coral polyps extend tentacles to feed voraciously on plankton, which contains in its tissues the one-celled zooxanthellae necessary to the polyps' growth. The formation that these corals will ultimately take—boulder-like, branching, or otherwise—depends on situational factors, including their location on the reef, the amount of available sunlight, the quality of the nutrient-rich waters to which they are exposed, and the protection they receive from wave action.

Filter-Feeders. The biodiversity of reef life in Malaysian Borneo is unmatched anywhere in the world. Plankton, the most important link in the reef food chain, consists of plant-like phytoplankton and animal-like zooplankton. Especially dense in these waters, plankton gives rise to an abundance of what are called "filter-feeders," animals with the ability to sift or snare plankton from the water column, including soft corals, mollusks, anemones, crinoids, gorgonians, and sponges. Plankton also contains larval forms of many fish and invertebrates, which ultimately hatch to become the reef's swimming or stationary inhabitants.

Soft corals and gorgonions are possibly the most beautiful animal creatures on the reefs of Sabah. Soft corals, as their name suggests, lack the hard limestone skeletons of reef-building hard corals; they grace, but do not build, the reef. The most spectacular soft coral is the rainbow-hued *Dendronephthya* (pp. 86,87). Gorgonion corals, also known as sea fans, thrive in a great variety of sizes, shapes, and colors in the waters of Sabah. As filter-feeders, they grow outward from walls and outcroppings, maximizing water flow along their prominent branches which, in turn, provide great surface areas for filtration. Some gorgonions grow to more than twelve feet across, and often you can see the tiny invertebrates, such as shrimp, crabs, or small fishes, that dwell in their folds (p. 8). Other corals that filter-feed include the smaller corals—such as mushroom, flower, and *Tubastrea*—as well as the larger black corals, such as whip corals and fire corals.

Sea anemones, despite their soft tentacles, are more closely related to hard corals than to soft corals. They come in a magnificent range of shapes and colors. They are known for their nematocysts (stinging cells), which they use to kill fish and invertebrates. Despite this, anemones provide homes for clownfish and porcelain crabs, which are immune to and protected by the stinging tentacles of the host anemone (pp. 21,47,183). Corallimorpharians, which look like anemones, have characteristics of both hard corals and anemones. A beautiful example of corallimorphs decorating a *Cyclocoeloma* crab is seen in this book (p. 66).

Sponges, the best known of the filter-feeders, are represented by an estimated 800 species in the waters here; a staggering number compared to the other oceans of the world. The reefs here are literally covered with a variety of forms including tubes, vases, and barrel sponges. Filter-feeders—such as crinoids (also known as feather stars)—perch on sponges as they filter plankton, while fish—such as butterflyfish and angelfish—feed on them directly. Sponges also offer hiding places for invertebrates, such as shrimp and crabs (pp. 18,71).

Invertebrates. Also living on the reef are flatworms, ribbonworms, segmented worms, and a huge variety of mollusks or shellfish. As members of the phylum Mollusca, these invertebrate animals have the ability to produce a calcareous shell, with the exception of the nudibranchs and cephalopods. Nudibranchs (or sea slugs) often appear in striking, even garish colors, which may warn predators that the animal is foul-tasting or poisonous (p. 19a). Cephalopods, including the octopus, squid, cuttlefish, and chambered nautilus, have highly developed eyes and sophisticated behaviors, making them efficient reef predators (pp. 16,58,78,84,188). It is the specialized pigment-containing cells called chromatophores that allow octopus, squid, and cuttlefish to instantaneously change colors in response to their environment. A dramatic example of this can be seen in the highly venomous blue ringed octopus depicted in this book (this page, p. 63).

Crustaceans, like the insects and spiders that are their cousins on land, make up the largest phylum of underwater animals. Many of these animals, including crabs, lobsters, and shrimp, remain hidden during the day and are only seen at night as they forage on the reef. Many commensal shrimp, as seen in this book, can be found living within anemones, corals, and sea urchins for protection (pp. 20,22,32,55,61). Cleaner shrimp, which remove parasites and dead tissue from fish, are also common (pp. 57,73). Crabs, which exist in huge numbers and varieties on the coral reef, are rarely seen before dark; during the day, they would be readily

eaten. Porcelain crabs (p. 21, 47), which live in a commensal relationship with anemones, have seines that they use to strain and filter plankton from the water. Probably the most interesting of all the crabs are decorator crabs, so named because of the way they attach living sponges, corals, and tunicates to their bodies for camouflage (p. 74). In the process, they become some of the most attractive and fascinating creatures on the reef.

Blue ringed octopus

Starfish, sea urchins, brittle stars, crinoids, and sea cucumbers comprise the phylum of Echinodermata, animals possessing a skeleton of spiny plates and five-part radial symmetry. Displaying a wide palette of colors, crinoids perch on gorgonions and sponges by holding on with small legs. They use more than thirty delicate arms to strain plankton from the water. The more plankton-rich the waters, as in Sabah, the greater the number and variety of crinoids.

Like crinoids, sea urchins rarely venture out during the day, but come out in huge numbers to feed along the reef at night. These aggressive grazers play an important role in the reef's ecology, since they are well-suited for scraping and removing algae and coral polyps from the reef. Sea cucumbers move slowly across the reef as they sift organic detritus from sandy areas. Although they have been harvested in huge quantities in many parts of the world, thankfully, this is not a problem in Malaysian Borneo.

Fish. Brilliantly colored fishes are the most spectacular and conspicuous inhabitants of the coral reefs. Some of the important groups seen in Sabah's waters are the bony fishes, such as eels, needlefish, squirrelfish, pipefish and seahorses, barracudas, damselfish and anemonefish, groupers, snappers, cardinalfish, coralfish and butterflyfish, angelfish, wrasses, parrotfish, sweetlips, blennies, rabbitfish, surgeonfish and unicornfish, scorpionfish and lionfish; batfish, boxfish, sweepers, red mullet and goatfish, and gobies. If other groups of fish are included (many of these are yet to be identified), it can be said that the number of fish species in Sabah's marine ecosystem may emerge as among the highest in the world.

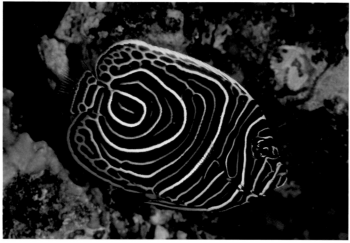

Juvenile emperor angelfish

Like other animals, fish are attracted to coral reefs for food, shelter, and reproduction. Some species remain deeply entrenched in the complex reef structures, effectively hiding there (pp. 49,53). Others conceal themselves during the day and emerge at night (pp. 24,68,80). Some species visit the reef temporarily, but do so frequently. All these behavior patterns cause difficulties in sampling and necessitate exhaustive studies. Greater efforts should be undertaken to survey, sample, and taxonomically identify as many new species as possible.

In addition to the tremendous diversity of bony fishes described above, there are many cartilaginous fishes, such as sharks and rays, seen on or near Sabah's reefs. Among the numerous species of sharks, the most common is the whitetip reef shark, which grows to about five feet. When not free-swimming, it can be seen sitting on sandy areas beneath coral overhangs and in caves (p. 190). Gray reef and black-tip reef sharks are also commonly seen; thresher and tiger sharks are less common. Whale sharks, the largest fish in the world, grow to forty feet long and are often found straining the plankton-rich waters off Sabah's coast. Giant manta rays, measuring up to twenty feet across and weighing more than 2,500 pounds, are also regular visitors to these waters where they, too, harmlessly strain plankton (p. 227).

Behavioral diversity among fish is also remarkable. Some fish operate individually, while many live in isolated schools or shoals (pp. 88,182,189). Often, small shoals of similar species merge to form bigger shoals, and bigger shoals split to form smaller ones. Like great flocks of birds underwater, the near-seamless coordination of movement of shoal members as they turn in unison is truly striking.

Fish live not only outside the reefs but also inside them; they are found almost everywhere in the reef's nooks and crannies, crevices, caves, fissures, overhangs, and tunnels (pp. 34,186). These special locations within the reefs provide an abode for small (and occasionally large) species, including damselfish, butterflyfish, angelfish, parrotfish, wrasses, and groupers. The coexistence of so many species, in such dense aggregation, is indeed surprising. Either these fish each have their specialized niche (to prevent antagonistic interaction) or an intricate mechanism of equilibrium exists that successfully maintains their diversity despite competition. A high level of opportunistic feeding in the predominantly carnivorous reef ichthyofauna can be one strategy to exist in an environment teeming with life. Use of the coral reef ecosystem alternately by diurnal and nocturnal species might serve to maximize use of the reef habitat, while avoiding negative interaction or competition. The importance of fish to the fragile ecology of the reef cannot be overstated. If they are depleted, or if they disappear, their absence will compromise the capacity of coral reefs to maintain their functional and structural integrity.

Nowhere is this structural integrity more graphically

portrayed than in the symbiotic interdependence that binds many different animals in the reefs. For example, the relationship of the sand goby and the blind cleaner shrimp is a mutually beneficial one (pp. 30,31). The shrimp, which cleans the goby's burrow, always maintains contact with the goby through its long antennae. The goby, in turn, signals warning of approaching predators, thus protecting the shrimp. Another form of symbiosis, commensualism, is demonstrated by the relationship of the clownfish and the anemone in which it makes its home. The clownfish clearly receives protection and nutrition from the anemone, while the benefit to the anemone is unclear and, perhaps, nonexistent. An even stranger form of symbiosis is demonstrated by the crustaceans and mollusks that go about their normal activities with corals, echinoderms, or ascidians attached to their bodies. Many examples of these symbiotic relationships are depicted in the photographs here (pp. 14,21,32,40,60).

Protecting the Reefs

Coral reefs are valuable for many reasons. Because reefs are found primarily in shallow waters, they act as natural barriers to waves, thereby protecting the shoreline from erosion, while creating a calm boating and diving environment to be utilized by tourists, professionals, and scientists. In the Malaysian reefs, as in few other places on the planet, the diversity of marine life is astoundingly rich, displaying natural beauty, as well as offering a wealth of raw materials that may someday be used to develop medicines and other commercial products. If conducted responsibly, marine ecotourism could provide new economic opportunities for local communities and help to sustain the environment, while at the same time decreasing the dependence of the populace on depleting activities, such as commercial fishing.

In recent years, the Malaysian government has demonstrated genuine concern about the conservation and sustainable exploitation of marine resources. Today, coral reefs are high on the conservation agenda, with legislation in place to curb unsustainable methods of exploiting marine resources,

and with the means of enforcement constantly under review. There is a growing need to protect the marine environment from human impact, to develop an effective means of managing coral reef fisheries, and perhaps to someday create effective medicines and other products from the reef's many resources. To accomplish these goals, we need to shift from a paradigm of resource management to one of systems management, from a focus on the conservation of a species to a focus on the conservation of habitat. We must work together to adopt a holistic, cooperative approach.

Stony corals

Overleaf: Spine cheek anemonefish

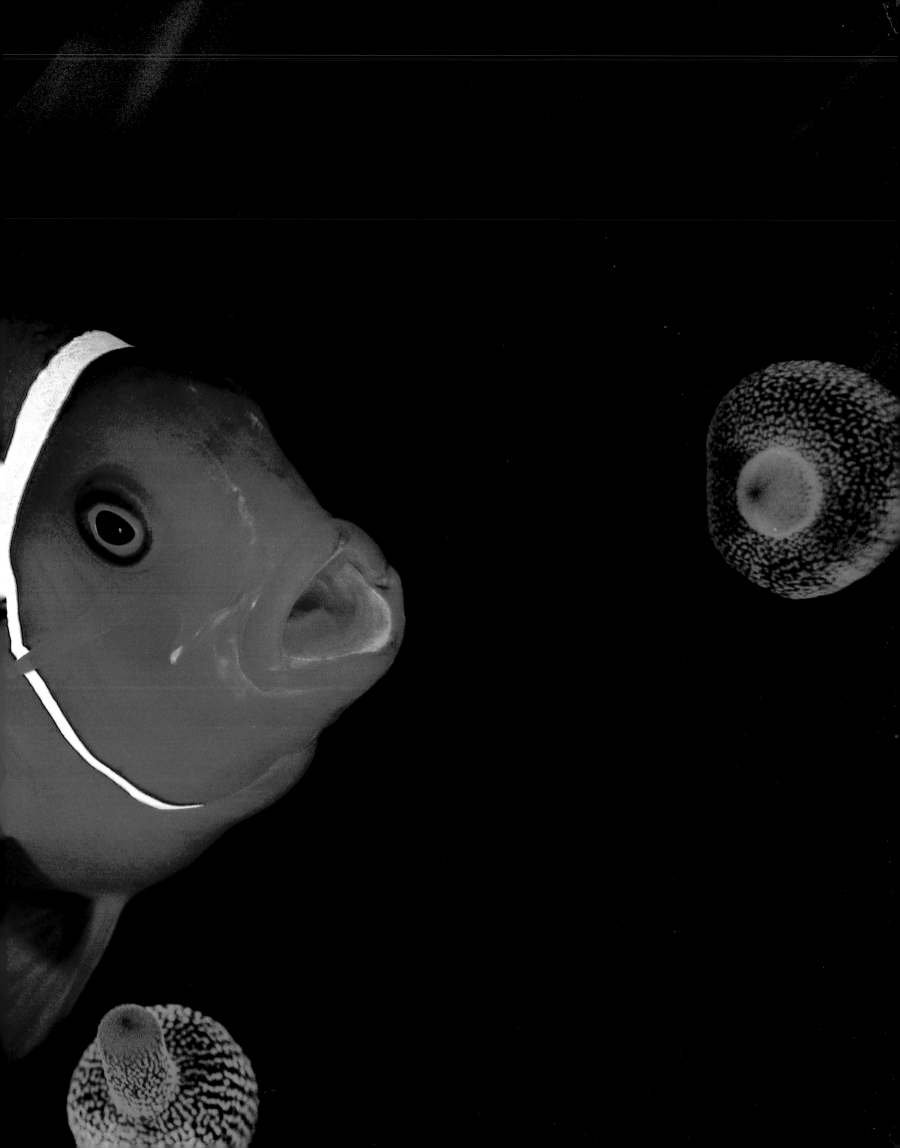

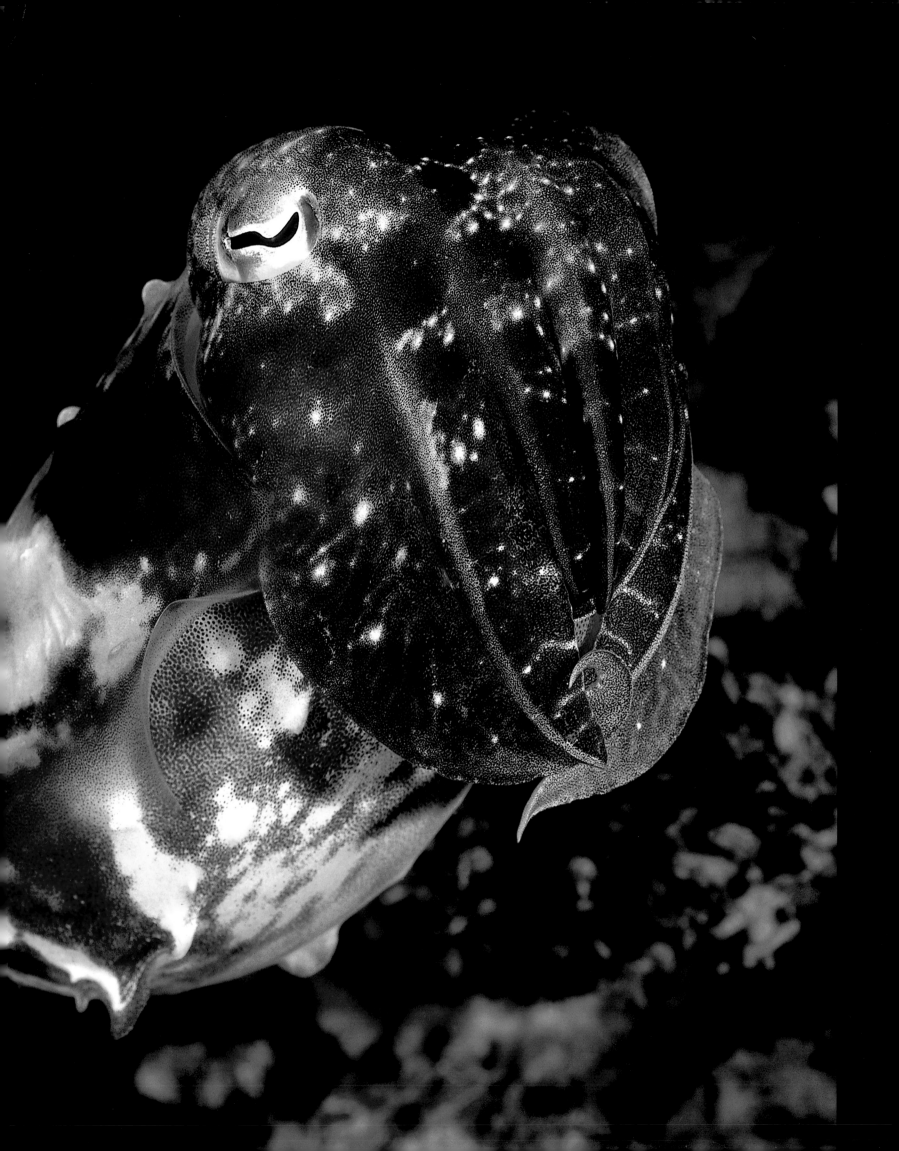

te: Broadclub cuttlefish

Mating broadclub cuttlefish

Left: Squat lobster

Opposite top: Nudibranch

Opposite bottom: Flatworm

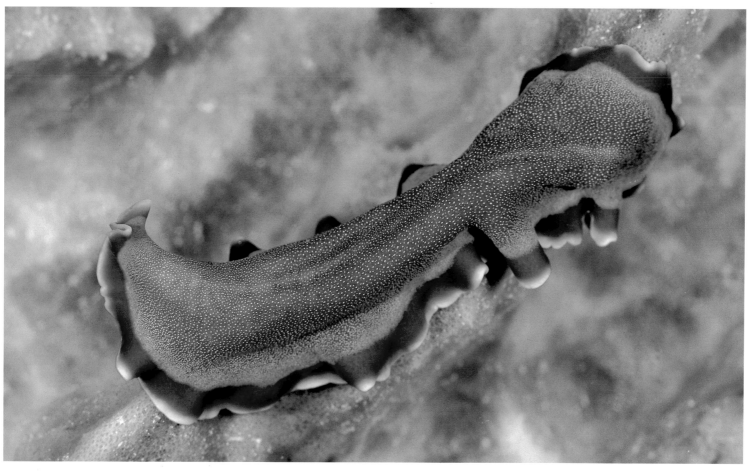

Opposite: Needle shrimp in a sea urchin

Above: Porcelain crab in host anemone

Commensal shrimp in hard coral polyps

Little file fish

Overleaf: Zebra lionfish

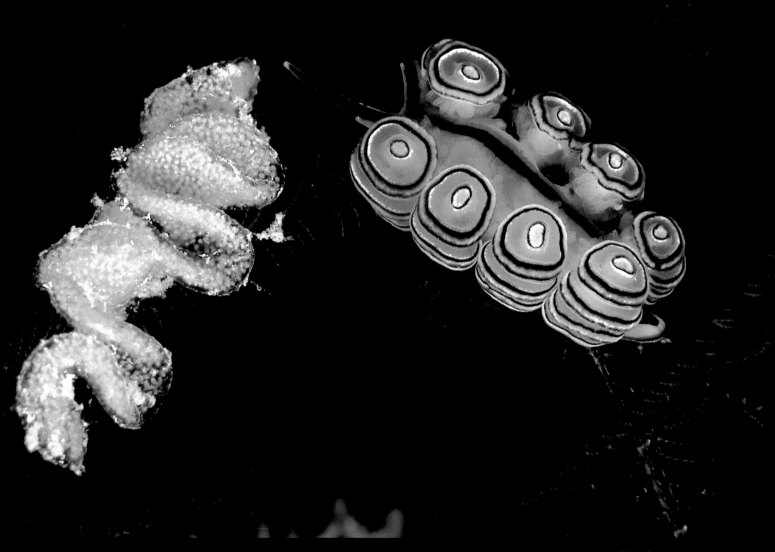

Nudibranch with eggs on stinging hydroids

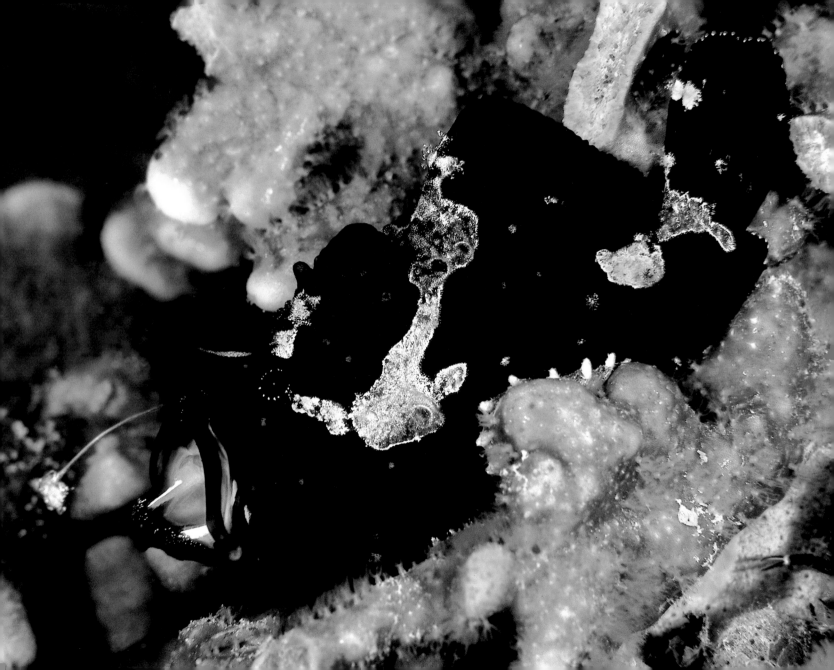

Top: Black rayed shrimp goby

Bottom: Black sailfin goby

Top: Spike-fin goby

Bottom: Rayed shrimp goby

Ambonion shrimp

Purple coral goby

Overleaf: Golden sweepers

Metallic shrimp goby

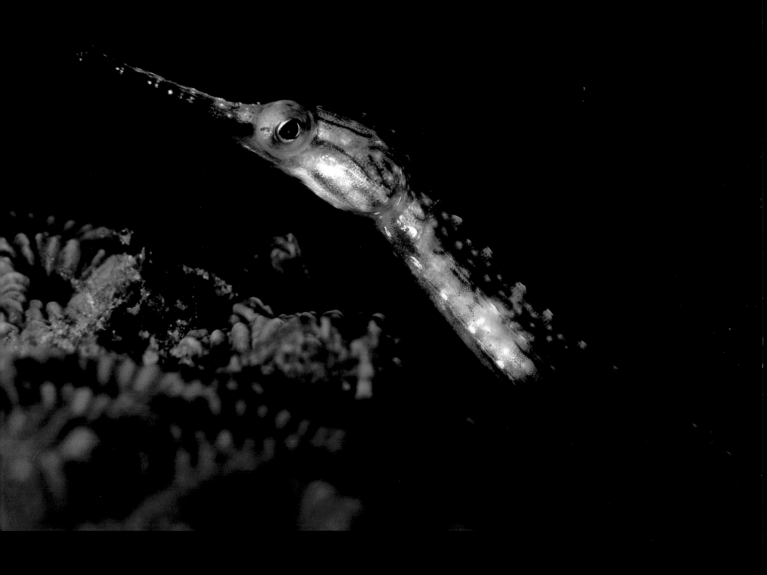

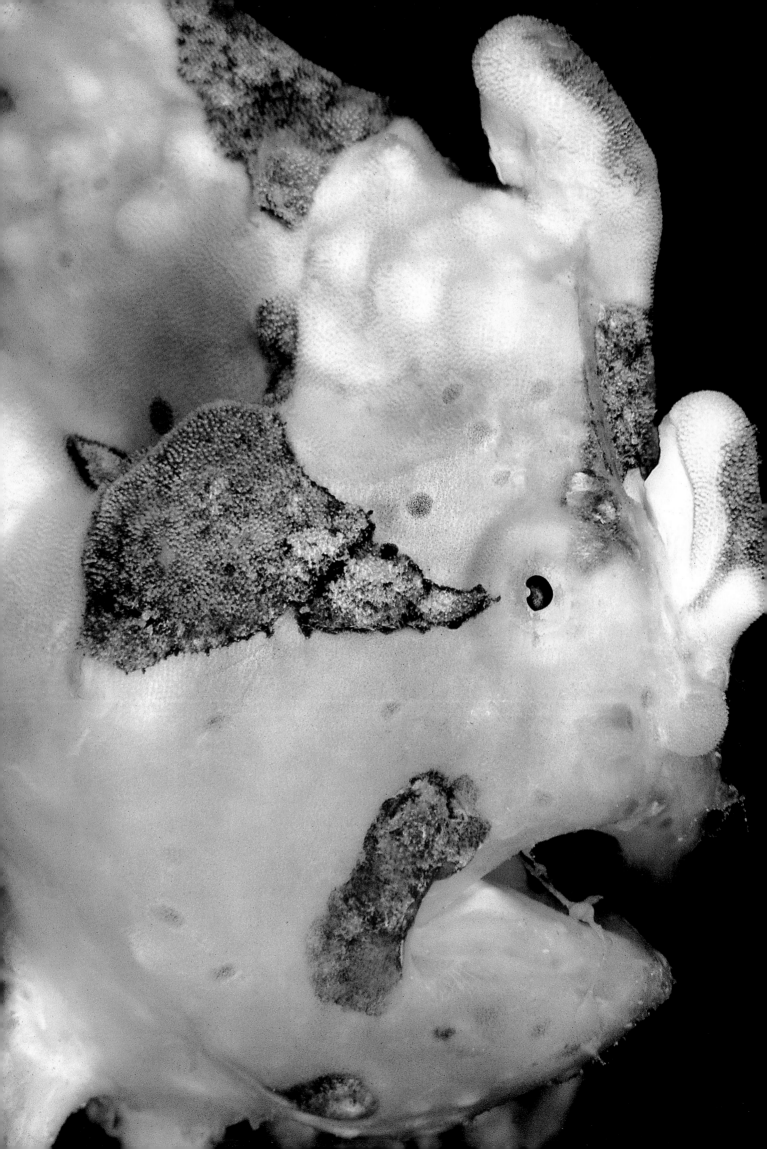

Opposite: Clown anglerfish

Above: Purple fire dartfish

Opposite: Porcelain crab
in a sea pen
Right: Cling goby guarding
eggs on a tunicate
Overleaf: Juvenile cardinalfish
in soft coral

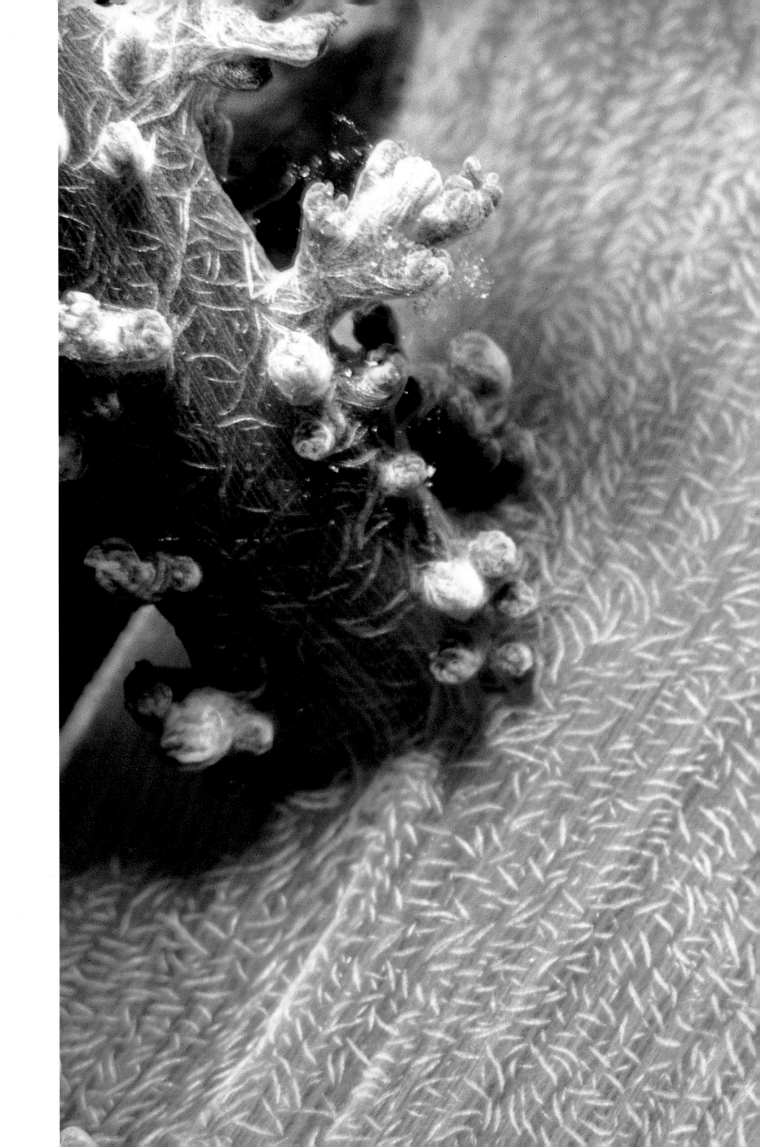

Alarmed

Bobtail Squid

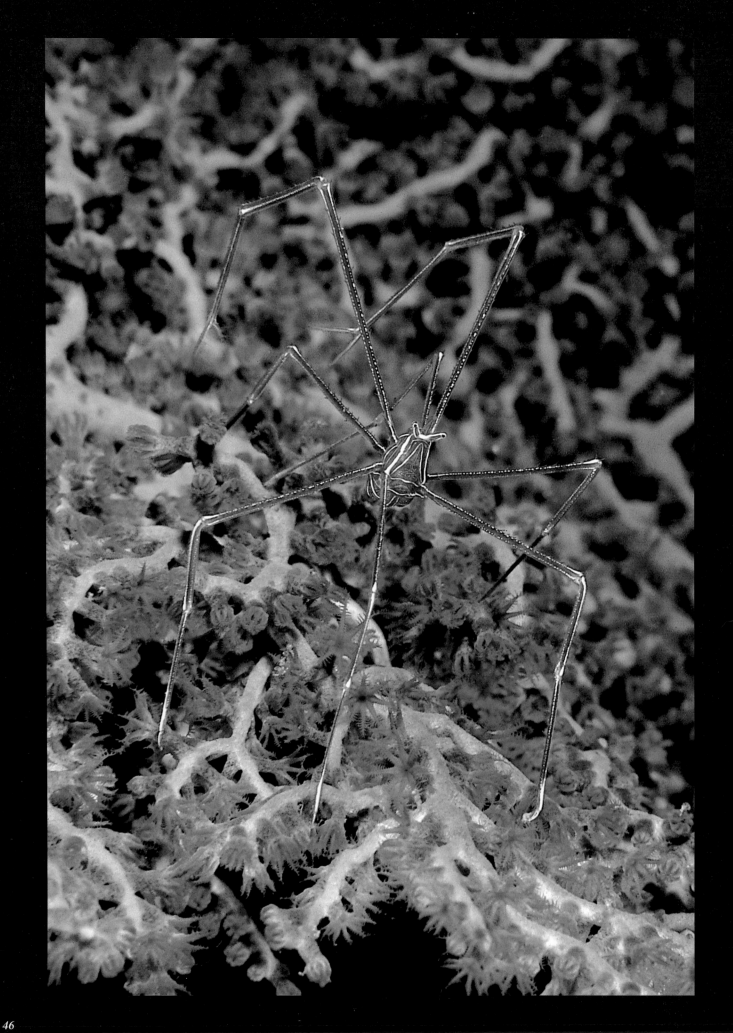

Opposite: Arrow crab on octocoral

Above: Spotted porcelain crabs

Above: Ribbon eel
Opposite: Mating mandarinfish
Overleaf: Schooling bumphead parrotfish

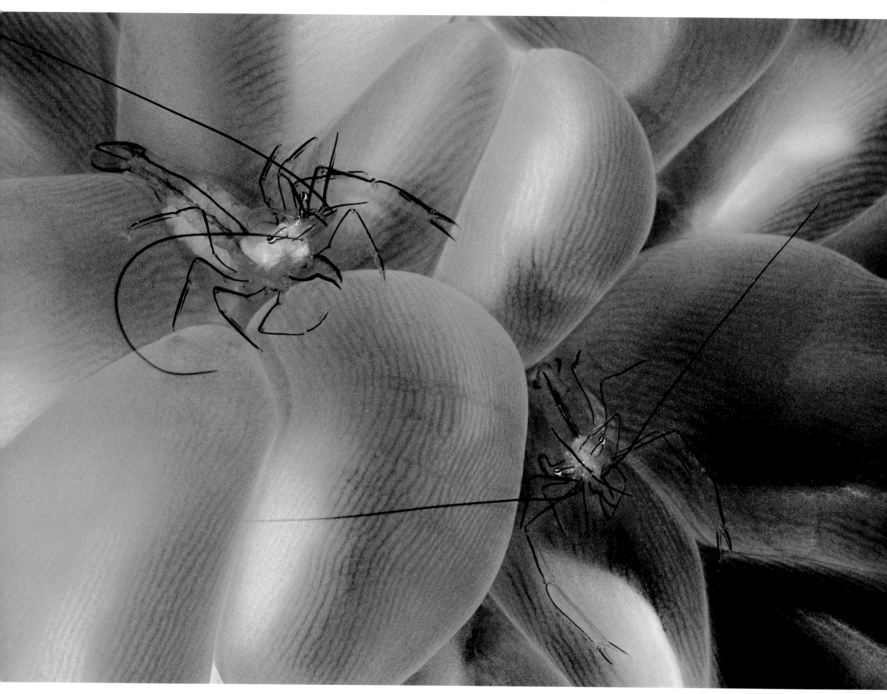

Opposite: Splendid garden eel

Above: Shrimp in bubble coral

Above: Banded sea krait

Opposite: Black spotted moray eel

Above and opposite: Flamboyant cuttlefish

Above: Featherstar clingfish
Opposite: Black wire coral shrimp

60

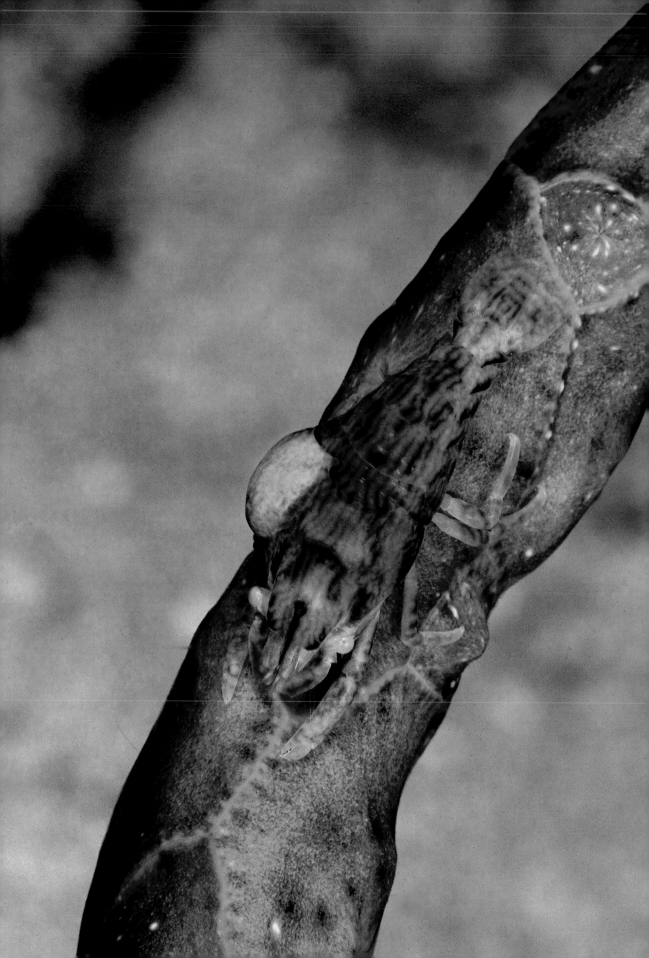

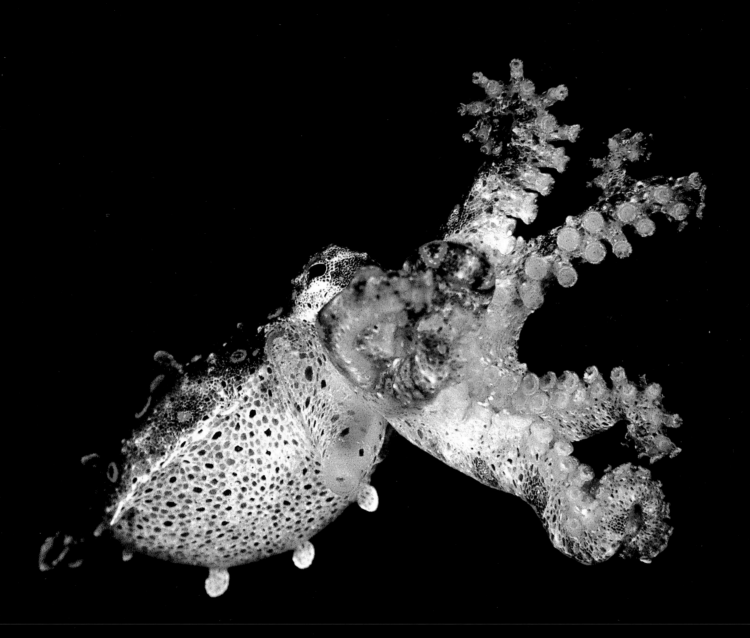

Opposite: Scribbled pufferfish eye
Above: Blue ringed octopus
Overleaf: Thorny sea horse

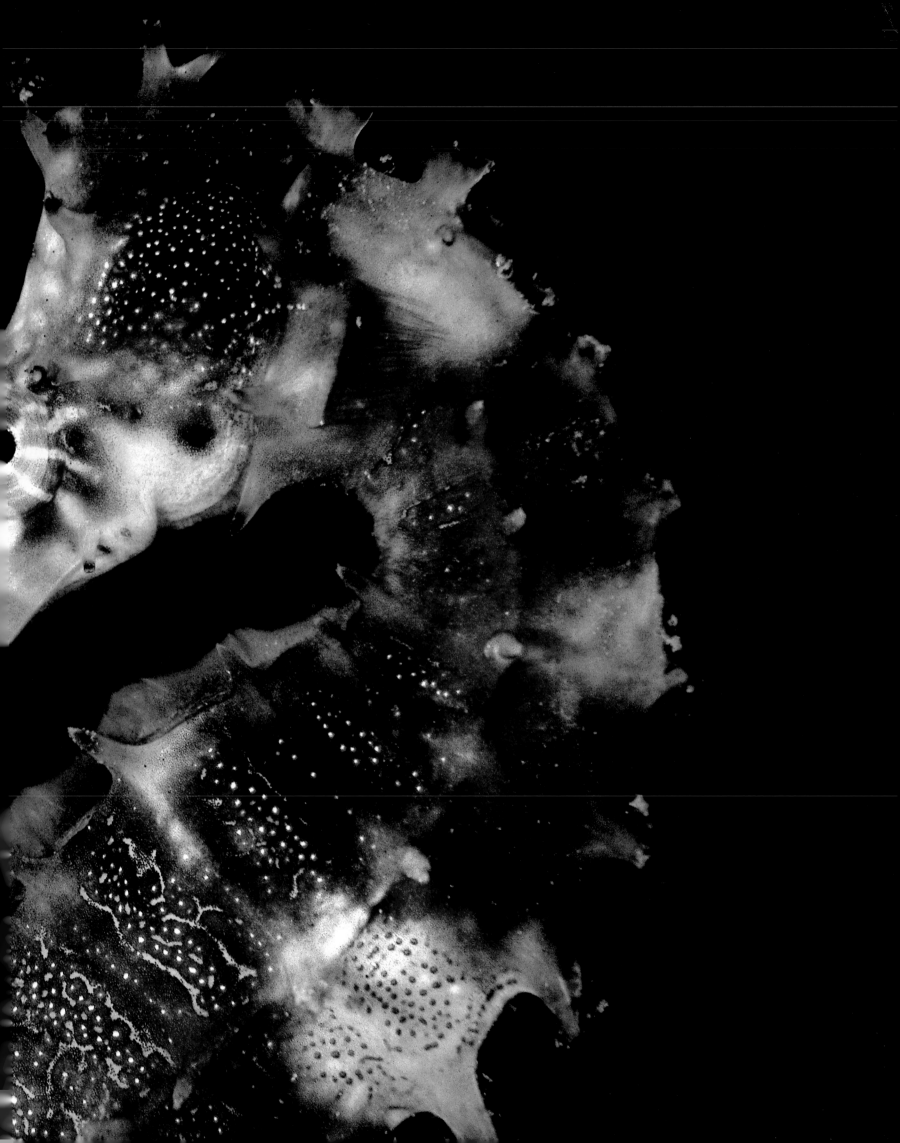

Opposite: Decorator crab

Above: Decorator crab in colonial coral

Left: Feather dus

Opposite: Squat

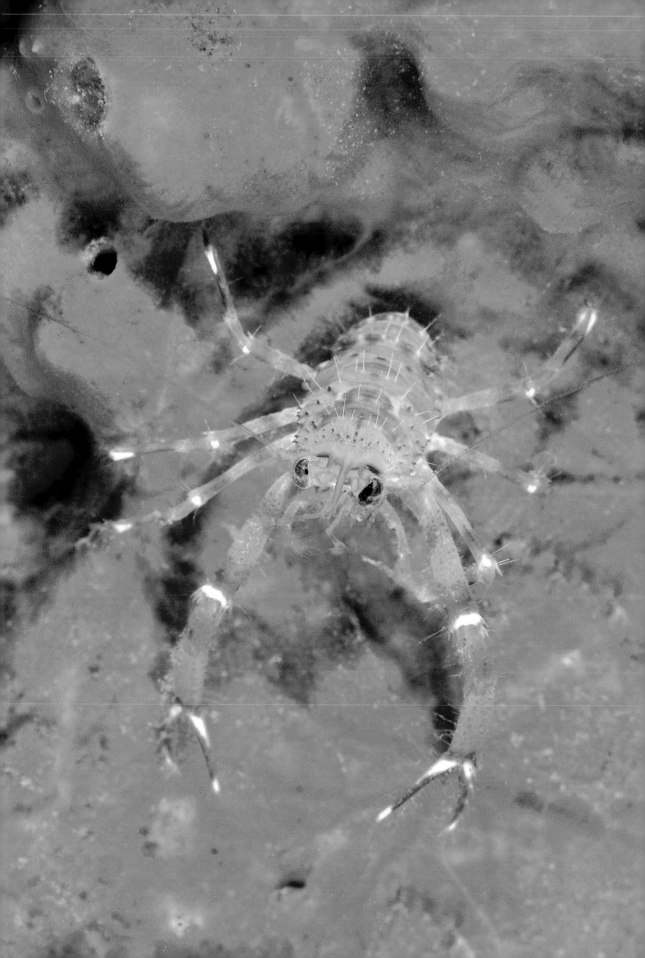

Left: Commensal shrimp
on a sea pen
Opposite: Leopard grouper with
cleaner shrimp

Opposite: Decorator crab in soft coral

Above: Flame file shell

Overleaf: Variable thorny oyster

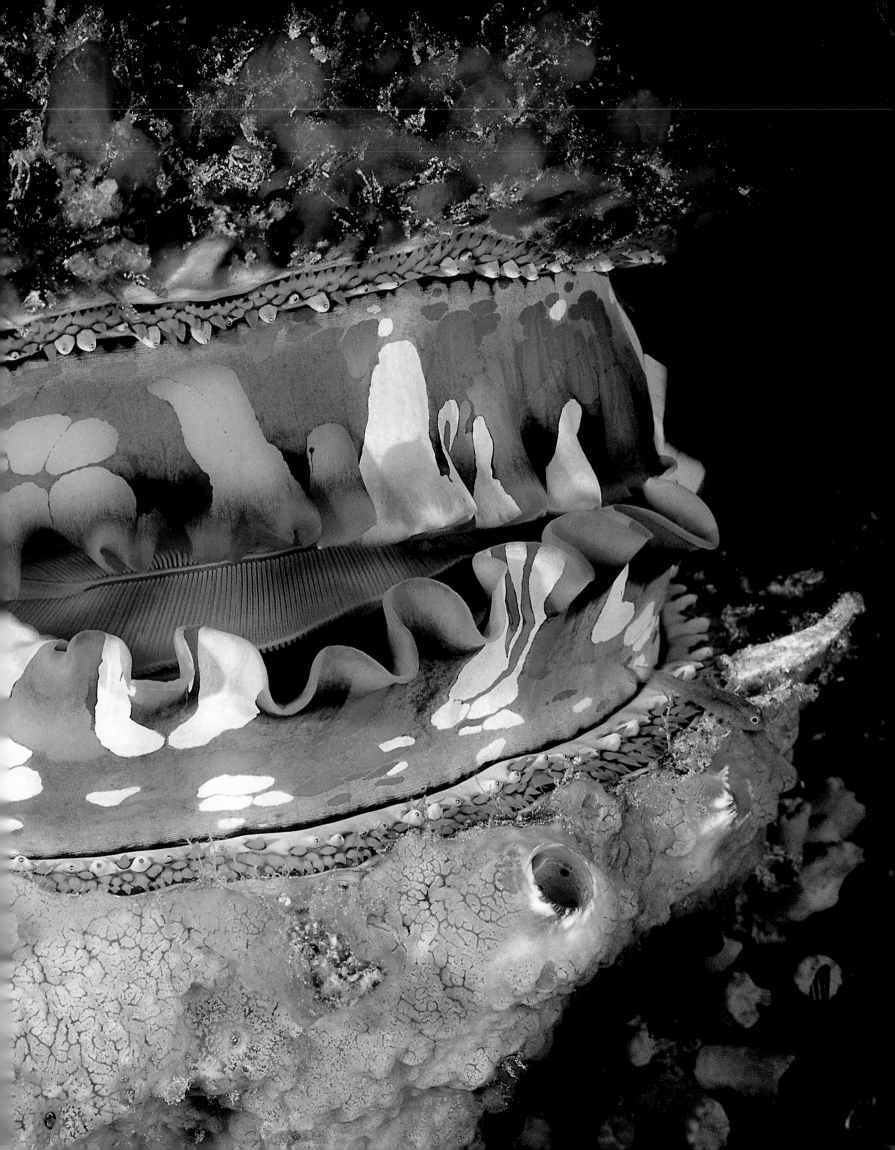

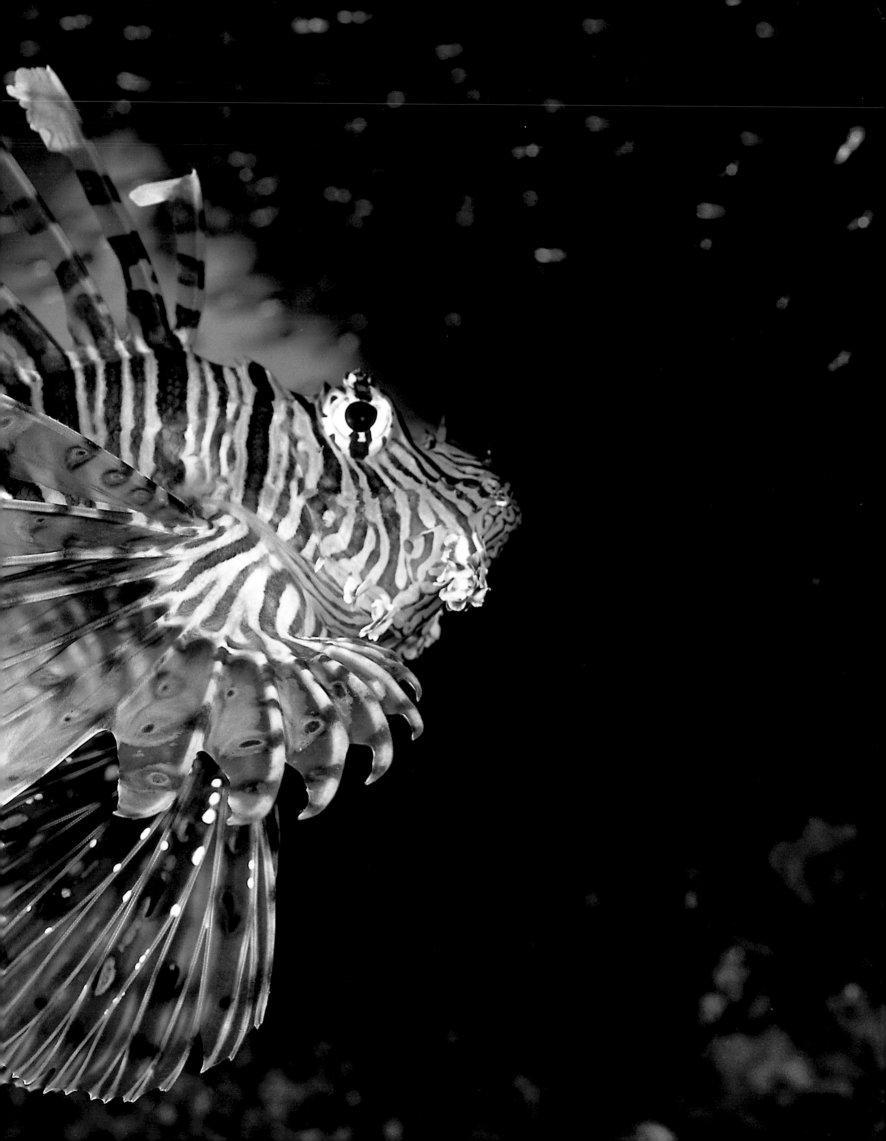

Top: Emperor Angelfish
Bottom: Regal Angelfish

Above: Bigfin reef squid

Opposite: Jellyfish with juvenile trevally jack

Opposite and right: Reef scenics
Overleaf: Schooling trevally jacks

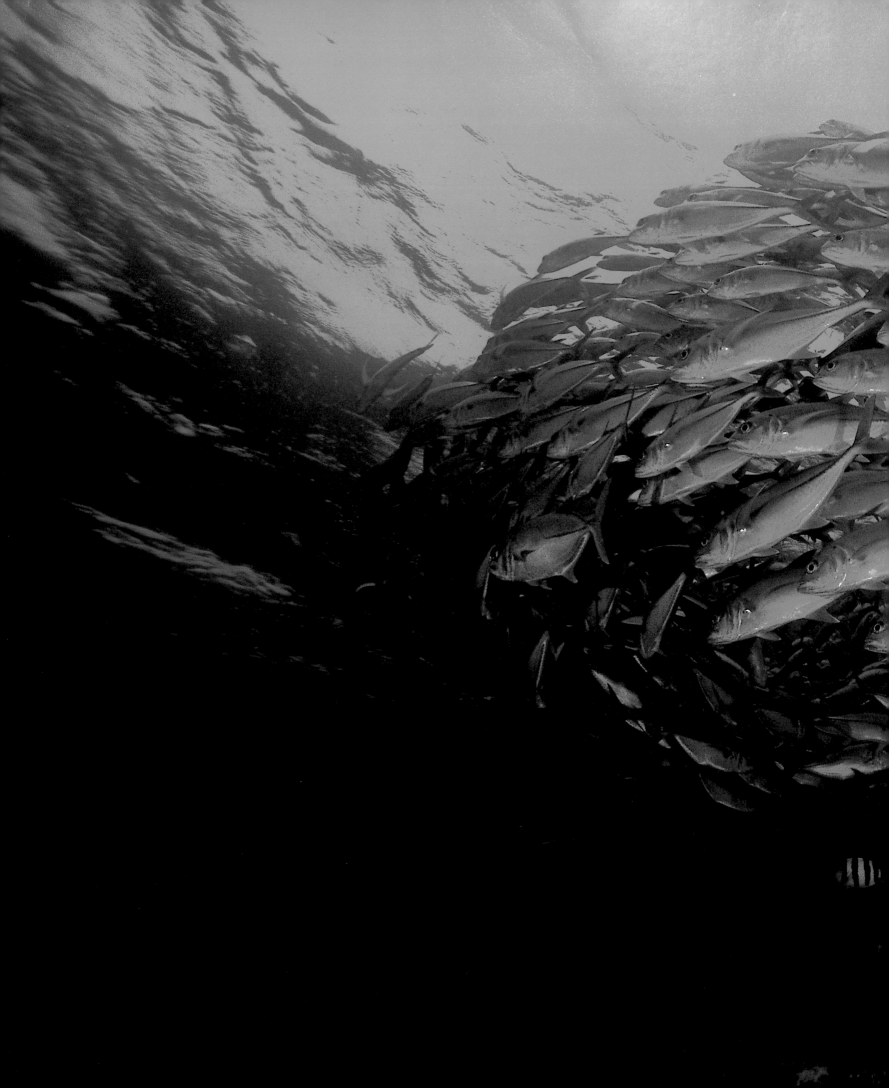

Rain Forests

Rain Forests

K.M. Wong, Ph.D.
Professor and Head
Rimba Ilmu Botanic Garden, Institute of Biological Sciences
Universiti of Malaya, Kuala Lumpur

Borneo's rain forests are part of the second largest region of rain forests in the world, after South America. This area of about 9,700 square miles, sometimes called the Indo-Malayan Rain Forest Region, is concentrated in the Malay Archipelago, which includes the Malay Peninsula, Sumatra, Java, Borneo, the Philippines, Sulawesi, Maluku, and New Guinea. It extends north and west to parts of Indochina, Thailand, Burma, Assam, Sri Lanka, the Western Ghats of India, and into the southwest Pacific on a narrow coastal strip in northeastern Australia. Borneo is the largest island on the Sunda continental shelf.

The term "tropical rain forest" was coined by the German botanist, A.F.W. Schimper, who first used Tropische Regenwald to describe the rich forests, principally around the equator, where temperatures vary less than five degrees Celsius between the warmest and coldest months and where average rainfall exceeds 100 inches per year. To early explorers, the loftiness and evergreen nature of the rain forest—with some formations reaching heights of 100 to 150 feet and with most trees maintaining a leafy crown throughout the year— were its most striking characteristics. Today, as we explore deeper into the rain forest, its intense species richness and the unique characteristics of its plant and animal life are far more captivating. Together with coral reefs, tropical rain forests are the richest ecosystems on Earth.

Life in the Rain Forest

An equable climate, in which plant growth is more or less continuous, is only one factor contributing to the richness of the Bornean rain forest. Fortuitously located at the point where the two great land masses of Asia and Australia separated from each other, Borneo was in a position to gain organisms from both continents. It is part of a great and complex archipelago in which the isolating effects of individual islands have nurtured specially adapted organisms. Some scientists speculate that the Malaysian rain forest could have existed as long as 140 million years ago, a significant portion of its plants and animals unaffected by the climatic changes of the Pleistocene Ice Age. The great topographic complexity of the high mountain ranges and stream-dissected terrain, as well as the diverse soils (derived from sandstone, coastal sand terraces, shale, peat, limestone, granite, basalt, and ocean crustal material), have also contributed to the numerous specially adapted species.

The term biodiversity refers to the totality of all species of organisms, including fungi, plants, animals, and their genetic variations, in a given area. The species richness, or biodiversity, of Bornean forests, although still far from being completely documented, is nonetheless astounding. For example, the British Isles have 1,430 species of native seed plants, while Borneo, with a land area only 2.4 times bigger, is thought to have over 12,000 species! In a more localized example, ecologists studying a 128-acre plot of rain forest in Lambir (Sarawak) found some 1,200 species of trees, represented by 360,000 stems. A comparable 123-acre plot in subtropical Panama had a mere 306 tree species, represented by 238,000 stems. In Malaysian Borneo (Sabah and Sarawak) alone, there are an estimated 3,500 tree species, of which between a quarter and a third are probably found nowhere else in the world. In comparison, the entire continent of Europe north of the Alps and west of Russia has only 50 native tree species; eastern North America has only 171.

That so many species can thrive together is a function of the rain forest's inherent nature. In addition to variation on the forest floor, there is also vertical variation with increasingly brighter, hotter, and drier conditions as you move up from the well-shaded earth floor into the forest canopy. This immense variety of living spaces and conditions (habitats) allows a plurality of forms to exist. Different organisms occurring together in one place, such as in a patch of forest, can continue to survive only if there is some kind of balance in the ways they obtain or use resources (i.e., light energy, a particular nutrient, or water). The specific function and position of each organism in the community is referred to as a niche. The scope and stature of the rain forest, with complex partitioning of space among many types of trees, gives rise naturally to a great many such niches. The organisms that fit into these niches include both specialists and generalists.

Orchid, *Renanthera bella*

Trees and Plants

Mixed-species lowland forest includes tropical heath, montane, mangrove, peat swamp, and fresh water swamp forest—all of them built on rich sandy clay. Some of the biggest trees here emerge beyond the general forest canopy to reach nearly 200 feet. At 285 feet, a single menggaris tree (from the legume or bean family) documented by Sabah's Forest Research Centre in 1995, appears to be the fifth-tallest tree in the world. However, it is the Dipterocarp family of trees that gives Borneo's forests their general character. This single plant family, of which all members are resin-producing trees, is known throughout the world for its hardwood timber. In the forests of the Malay Archipelago, especially in Borneo, Dipterocarps are among the largest trees, with 268 species in the Borneo lowlands alone.

In addition to trees, other life forms abound. Plants in the rain forest include a rich diversity of leafy herbs, shrubs, and climbers. Epiphytes (plants that grow non-parasitically on other plants) range from tiny algae covering leaf surfaces to huge masses of tiger orchids sitting atop the biggest trees; the largest of these in Malaysian Borneo is reputed to weigh in excess of two tons. There are also parasitic plants, including the *Rafflesia*, an extremely rare and bizarre plant without stems or leaves, which produces the largest blossom known in the plant kingdom. Several photographs of this hard-to-find flower appear in this book (pp. 160,161,197). There are saprophytes, plants also without leaves, which lack chlorophyll and absorb nutrients from decaying organic matter. They include the tiny, leafless *Thismia*, which bears miniscule flowers with tentacle-like appendages, and the orchid, *Aphyllorchis*. Such plants often depend on association with fungi, which supply metabolites to their delicate roots. Many trees in the Borneo rain forest, too, are "mycorrhizal," meaning that they depend on association with fungi to help increase the absorption of nutrients through their roots.

Often, the apparent stillness of the rain forest belies the vibrant life processes that it supports. For example, all thirty-one species of pitcher plants (*Nepenthes*) known in Borneo have peculiar, bowl-like structures at their leaf tips (pp.

170–72). These are used to catch (and digest) insects and small animals, but a number of other animals have adapted to living inside the pitchers or utilizing the enzyme-rich solutions they hold as a hunting ground. This so-called "infauna" includes frog tadpoles—which complete their metamorphosis from eggs deposited inside the pitchers—and some species of crabs. Similarly, certain groups of epiphytes that attach to tree stems and branches, including *Hydnophytum* and *Myrmecodia*, have swollen stem tubers riddled with interconnecting channels, forming a system of caves in which some ants live and breed, protecting and feeding their host with their excrement and debris. As in the reefs, signs of remarkable symbiosis are evident everywhere in the rain forest.

Perhaps one of the most fascinating plant groups is the orchids. In Borneo, there are over 1,500 species—more than anywhere else in the world—and their classification has challenged generations of specialists. Among many species known for their beauty is *Paphiopedilum rothschildianum*, the slipper orchid, which is also one of the rarest. Human activity and illegal collection have depleted this flower so that only a few natural populations are now known on Mount Kinabalu (p. 168). The flower has a central kinked appendage (staminode) covered with glandular hairs that apparently mimic an aphid colony and draws in some female flies to lay their eggs.

Another beauty is the *Renanthera bella* orchid, with intensely deep-red flowers (opposite page). This species, also much depleted from the wild by overcollecting, is still something of a mystery. Being an "epiphyte" (attached to another plant for support), it is difficult to explain why it might be endemic to sites with ultramafic geology, in other words, to soils rich in heavy metals, such as cobalt, magnesium, and nickel, but poor in the major nutrients most plants require (p. 208). Not all orchids are showy like the *Renanthera bella*. Smaller ones include some captivating forms, such as the group of species called helmet orchids which possess only a single leaf shaped like a small coin and a small, solitary flower (p. 234).

Animals

Borneo has over 220 species of forest mammals. The largest cat in the forest is the clouded leopard (p. xvi), but it is not as frequently encountered as the leopard cat (p. 142), which is active at forest fringes, plantations, and in gardens. The world's smallest bear, the sun bear (below), also lives in Borneo's forests and is industrious at locating bees' nests. Other large mammals include the Asian two-horned rhinoceros, the barking deer, and the Sambar deer—all herbivores (pp. 200, 122, 235, respectively).

Sun bear

Bearded pigs are normally quite localized; during some years, however, herds may migrate impressive distances within the forest as the Dipterocarp trees come into "gregarious" fruiting (i.e., all at once) at one location, followed closely by another gregarious fruiting further on, thus presenting a wave of available food for the pigs to follow. The Asian elephant is known only in Sabah and nearby Kalimantan; this fact, and the lack of fossil evidence, suggests that it was introduced in historically recent times, although this is not proven (p. 136). Rodents of the rain forest include tree squirrels, ground squirrels, flying squirrels, rats, and porcupines. Some squirrels use the woody climbers as aerial runways between tree branches and between levels.

Primates, which are mainly diurnal, utilize the upper levels of the rain forest where they can travel very rapidly. One of the most intriguing sounds in the forest is the loud "bubbling" territorial call of the female Bornean gibbon—a species which, like the orangutan, lacks a tail (i.e., they are apes; p. 100). Male orangutans, the largest tree-dwelling animals in the world, live mostly in fresh water swamp forests. They can roar loudly enough to be heard two miles away, possibly warding off other males and attracting females (pp.130,131,200,201, 204). Orangutans are highly solitary animals, except when pairing briefly (up to a week) for mating and when a mother cares for its young (up to three years). An orangutan requires a great deal of fruit—supplemented by honey, insects, and other foods—to maintain its body mass. A female produces a single offspring every three to eight years and appears to require a core area of at least 148 acres of forest all to herself.

A total of 622 bird species have been documented in Borneo, including 39 not known anywhere else and 188 considered migrant or vagrant. Indigenous birds are found mostly in montane forests. Three examples from the mountains of northwest Borneo show how diets and behavior vary between groups: the mountain serpent eagle feeds on snakes and lizards, Whitehead's trogon is insectivorous, and the mountain black-eye has a bill suited to consuming nectar from (and possibly pollinating) certain rhododendrons. The mountains of northwest Borneo, in particular Mount Kinabalu (at 13,455 feet, the highest peak between Indochina and New Guinea; p. 164), are famed for their abundant bird-watching possibilities.

Nocturnal Life

A different forest comes to life after dark. Once your eyes adapt to the darkness, you begin to see a faint, eerie, greenish-white light, which is the natural bioluminescence of usually invisible fungal strands, emanating from decaying twigs and branches on the forest floor (p. 113). The leaves of some plants, especially those of the bean family, "close" at night, folding their leaflets together. Frogs become much more obvious, at least by their sounds. In Borneo, there are some 150 frog species ranging from the Bornean horned frog—a common ground frog found throughout the lowlands up to about 4,800 feet—to tree frogs such as *Polypedates spp.*, which only descend from the trees to breed in stagnant pools (pp.

118,119,140,233, respectively). At night, the pangolin, a scaly, toothless mammal, hunts for ants and termites, as does the slow loris, a primate that feeds on fruits and insects (pp. 132,133, respectively). A truly peculiar creature, also active at night, is the Western tarsier, a diminutive primate not much larger than a kitten with ears, eyes, feet, and a tail that superficially resemble those of a bat, owl, frog, and rat, respectively, as can be seen in this book (pp. 110,114).

A nocturnal mammal that is somewhat more mobile than the slow loris and the tarsier is the colugo, which glides through the trees using a fold of skin that links its front and hind legs on each side of its body. Called the flying lemur, it does not actually fly and is not at all related to lemurs. Other gliding mammals include several species of so-called flying squirrels, which have skin flaps stretching between their fore and hind limbs much like the flying lemur. The flying frog, first illustrated in 1869 by naturalist Alfred Russel Wallace, a contemporary of Darwin, does not even properly glide, much less fly. Rather, it spreads out the webbed digits on all four of its limbs as it jumps from tree to tree.

Finally, in a spectacular prelude to their nocturnal foray, an estimated 1.8 million bats stream out of the Gomontong Cave each dusk. The power of true flapping flight allows bats to travel farther from their regular roosts, as with the large flying fox, a fruit bat that ranges from the inland forests to coastal areas and islands.

The Unknown

Even as Borneo becomes more inhabited and developed for agriculture and settlement, an aura of mystery remains. There are still wooded expanses untouched by human beings, although human activity continues to intrude farther into the forests. There is as of yet no complete modern listing of the flora, and not even a remotely comprehensive account of the trees, which are the most structurally significant elements of the rain forest. Many groups of herbaceous plants are yet to be carefully studied and classified, and each new study continues to reveal species previously unknown to science.

Of the many groups of organisms, insects remain the least known; in Borneo alone, specialists estimate some 3,000 to 4,000 varieties of moths. Scientists are using fogging and other sampling methods to count and catalogue insects. Within a sampling area of only a few trees, dozens of insect families have been discovered, including species never before seen or classified scientifically.

The mystery extends to the rain forest canopy, where studies of life and its processes have been, understandably, rare. Here is where the chemistry of defense employed by leaves against herbivores becomes paramount, and the search for plant chemicals with specialized effects on animal tissues, highly relevant. Orangutans, gibbons, and macaques have simple stomachs and cannot digest leaves to obtain energy; they must depend on sweet fruits and other food material. Leaf monkeys, on the other hand, have complex stomachs capable of bacteria-aided digestion of leaf cellulose, but cannot eat leaves with antibiotic properties, as they are detrimental to stomach bacteria (p. 128). Like proboscis monkeys, which are found mainly in Borneo's coastal forests, they eat non-sweet fruits (sweet fruits would cause bloat) and young, less-fibrous leaves that are easily broken down (pp. xiii,148,149). Insects, too, prefer some leaves while avoiding those containing toxins. Just as the rest of the rain forest, the canopy is a great battle-field for survival that remains largely unexplored.

Unfolding Perspectives

As far as we know, there are many species endemic to Borneo, some of them known, and many being discovered each day. For example, as many as 40 percent of the 290 species of palms in Borneo do not exist elsewhere in the world, and the same is true for more than 50 percent of the Dipterocarp trees. Of the snakes, 31 of 154 known species are not found outside the island (pp. 109,141).

Ecologists have also noted that many plant groups found in the same area of rain forest are represented not by just one, but often by many additional closely related species. For example, multiple species of the Dipterocarp genus *Shorea* can be encountered in Borneo while taking a walk through any patch of undisturbed lowland rain forest. Sometimes, this "sister-species" phenomenon is also observed on mountains. On Mount Kinabalu alone, there are 98 different species of figs and 46 species of oaks. Among animals in the forest, multiple species of the same genus co-occur frequently, especially among amphibians and insects. This phenomenon clearly reflects the active rate of speciation (species evolution) in rain forests, a result of the ability of different populations of organisms to fit into different niches. In other words, rain forests are power-houses of evolution, where many new variants and species are able to specialize and survive.

A final perspective that should be noted is that of species rarity. The species richness, or the ultimate number of different species, in Borneo rain forests is due to species that are exceedingly rare. The large number of rare species in the Borneo rain forests reminds us that is important to focus our conservation efforts on large areas and not just a few well-known sites if we wish to preserve this environment whose fragile balance and unmatched biodiversity still has much to teach us.

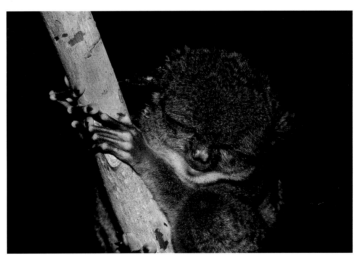

Sleeping tarsier

Overleaf: Strangling fig

Left: Bornean gibbon

Opposite: Climbing vine

Left: Buffy fish-owl

Opposite: Walker lanternflies

Left and opposite:
Pig-tailed macaques

Left: Rhinoceros hornbill

Opposite: Wreathed hornbill

e: Green tree lizard
umatran pit viper

Opposite: Western tarsier

Above: Rajah Brooke's birdwings

Opposite: Tree frog
Right: Luminous mushrooms
Overleaf: Western tarsier

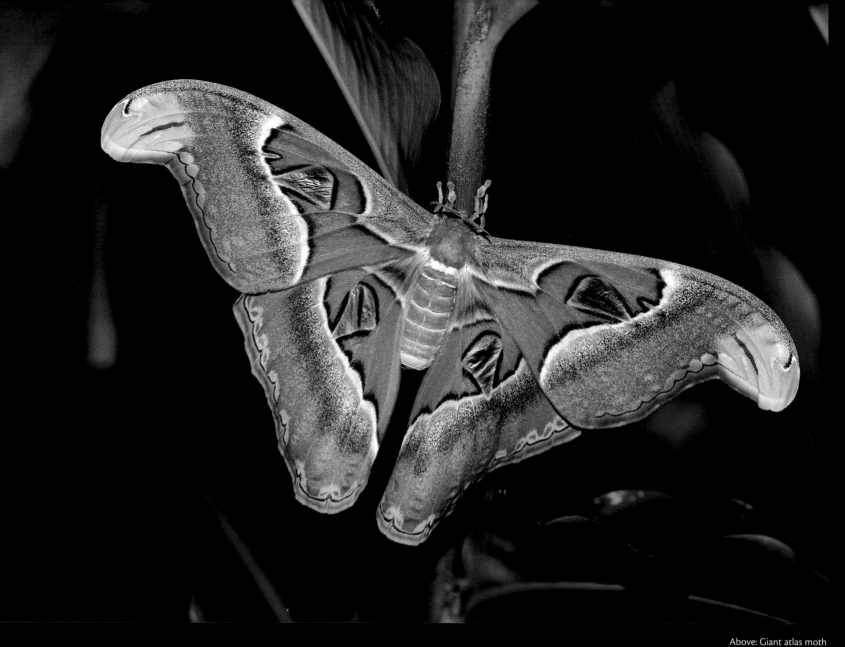

Above: Giant atlas moth

Opposite: Giant atlas moth (face)

Left: Bornean horned frog

Opposite: Camouflaged frog

Left: Millipede

Opposite: Pill millipede

Opposite: Barking deer
Right: Banded palm civet
Overleaf: Sunrise in the
Danum Valley

Left: Centipede

Opposite: Lichen spider

Left: Red leaf monkey
Opposite Bracket fungi

Opposite: Male orangutan

Above: Female orangutan with infant

Above: Pangolin

Opposite: Slow loris

Overleaf: Salt lick at Tabin Wildlife Refuge

Opposite: Asian elephant

Above: Binturong

Overleaf: Forest scenic

Opposite: Cinnamon tree frog

Above: Reticulated python

Opposite: Masked palm civet
Above: Leopard cat

Opposite: Comb-crested agamid lizard

Above: Bushy-crested hornbill

Overleaf: Sunrise, Kinabatangan River

Above: Adult male proboscis monkey

Opposite: Female proboscis monkey with infant

Opposite: Black and red broadbills

Above: Riverine rain forest scenic

Left: Blue-eared kingfisher

Opposite: Stork-billed kingfisher

Above: Horned spiders
Opposite: Dillenia flowers

154

Opposite: Juvenile purple herons

Above: Stick insect

Overleaf: Forest scenic

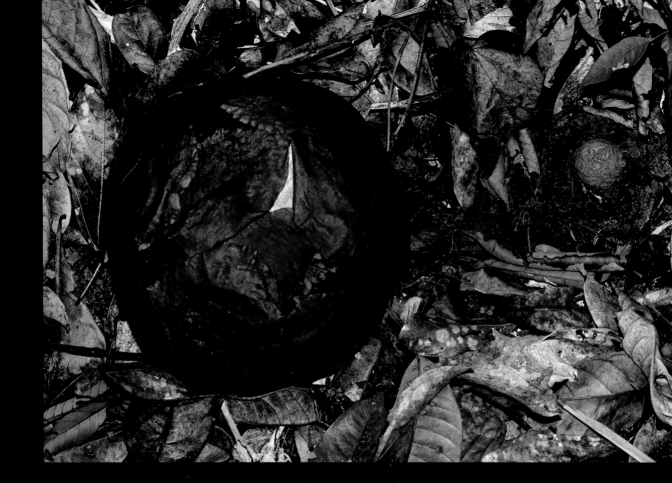

Top: *Rafflesia* buds
Bottom: *Rafflesia keithii*

Top: *Rafflesia pricei*
Bottom: *Rafflesia tengku-adlinii*

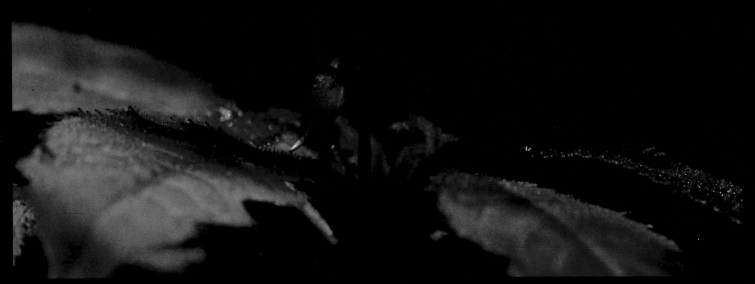

Kinabalu balsam

Lobelia

Opposite and right:
Pitcher plants

Opposite: Pitcher plant

Above: Trilobite beetle

Overleaf: Medinella

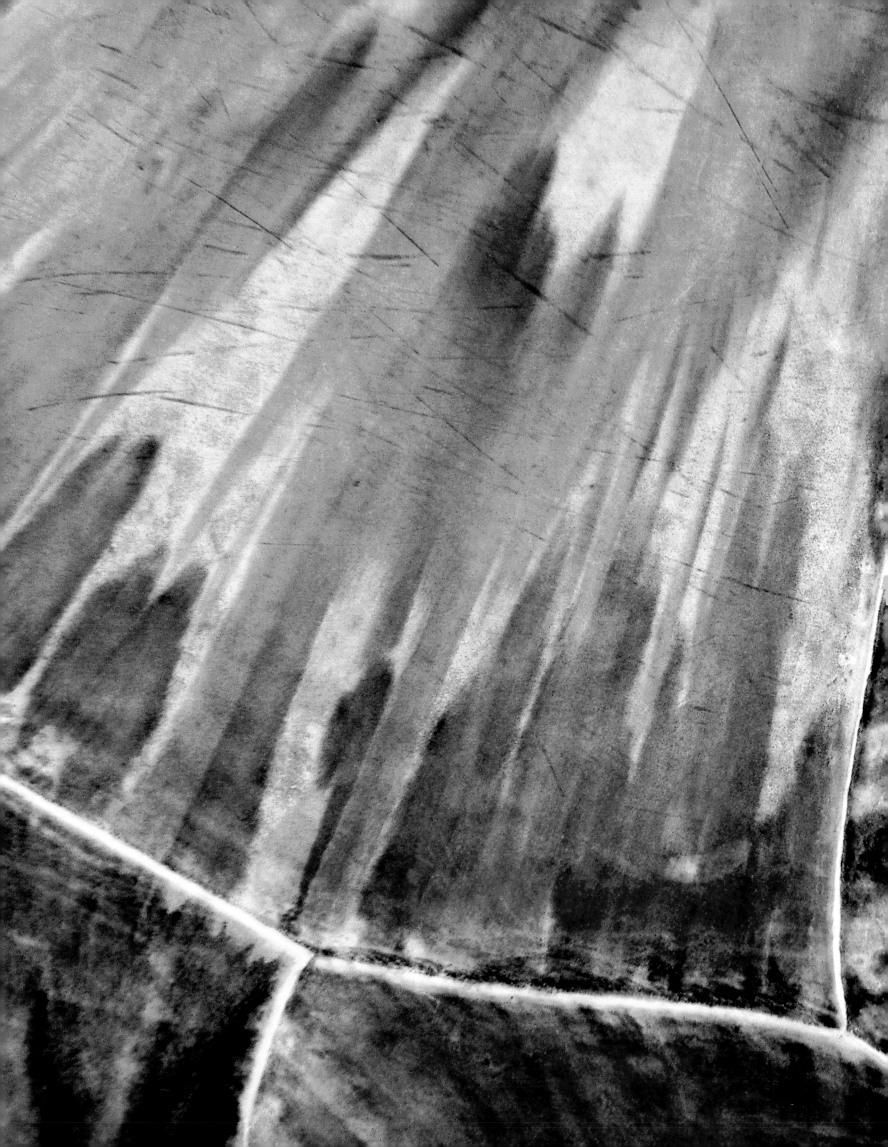

Regarding Conservation

Aerial walkway

Regarding Conservation

Tengku Datuk Dr. Zainal Adlin
Chairman, World Wildlife Fund Malaysia
Chairman, Sabah Tourism Promotion Corporation
Ministry of Tourism Development, Environment, Science and Technology, Sabah, Malaysia

Conservation is a vast topic. Simply put, conservation is the judicious use and management of natural resources for the benefit of human society and for ethical reasons. Much of conservation thinking is embodied in the concept of sustainable development, a concept based on the understanding that human well-being depends on the well-being of nature and the environment.

It is important that our activities in conservation remain focused. We seek especially to keep areas such as parks and watershed protection forests in pristine condition in order to protect natural biological populations, communities, and landscapes. Also important is reducing the degradation to natural systems that we do alter, for example, through the logging of forests or river use. Not least, because conservation involves people, the public must be made aware of the need for environmentally sustainable habits and for specialized studies of nature in threatened areas.

Habitat Conservation

The only effective way to have meaningful conservation in a region as rich as ours is through habitat conservation. Habitats, such as coral reefs and tropical rain forests, are threatened by destruction through human activities and population growth, and through gradual erosion as occurs when the area marked for conservation is too small. Loss of forest cover and coral destruction can be correlated with the rapid increase in human population and the large-scale, landscape-altering activities of people. So, even habitat conservation must go hand in hand with other strategies for sustainable development, including slowing down population growth and, in some cases, reducing the overabundance of tourism operators and tourists in the

most superb areas where their presence is of no advantage to the environment.

Special sites can be earmarked for specific protections— the creation of a park, nature monument, or wildlife sanctuary, for example, may be easier to deal with than the idea of conserving a "generic" lowland rain forest (pp. 134,194). For instance, Mount Kinabalu, considered to be one of the most important biological sites in Asia, is quite sensibly located within a park (p. 158). It is a natural attraction for anyone who wants to see the Far East, yet today Mount Kinabalu remains one of the true wild places of the tropics—its immense proportions and rugged landscape have not been anywhere near thoroughly explored. So, too, is Maliau Basin, Sabah's "Lost World," located within an almost circular basin hemmed in by steep sandstone ridges, in the south-central part of the state (p. 198).

Sabah and Sarawak are states where natural treasures abound, from rain forests to reefs. A little more than fourteen miles out to sea from Sabah's east coast are the greatest marine destinations of this part of the world: the Semporna Islands of Bodgaya, Boheydulong, and Tetagan. Nestled in sparkling waters between the Darvel Bay and the Sulawesi Sea, these islands rival any other ocean sites, including the great diving paradise of Sipadan Island. The Semporna Islands are unique in that they are remnants of the rim of a former volcano now mostly underwater. Attention has been refocused on the islands after surveys associated with the WWF (World Wildlife Fund) Malaysia "The Seas Must Live" campaign of 1977–78 highlighted their pristine condition and the rich coral reef life found in the lagoon and surrounding areas. The deep, clear waters and the increased land fringes offered by the Bodgaya Islands make an ideal marine life habitat. The reefs around the

Commensal shrimp on black coral

Semporna Islands have been mapped and their biologically significant characteristics recorded, making them one of the most thoroughly documented reef systems in Southeast Asia and considered to be the finest in Sabah's waters. In 1998, a team of marine biologists and ecologists discovered many unique aspects of the reefs and the native marine life, with many rare species worthy of conservation.

The Semporna reefs, surely one of Malaysia's national treasures, are as vulnerable as other reefs to damage through the use of heavy fishing boats and other destructive activities, such as dynamite fishing. What happens on land affects the reefs as well; land clearance and resulting soil erosion can lead to siltation in sheltered lagoons where wave action and currents are weaker, resulting in lowered rates of "flushing," ultimately choking the corals to death. Such are the natural subjects of conservation planning and, at present, the Semporna Islands are proposed for gazetting as a national park. With their spectacular landscapes and scenery, unusual plant communities, magnificent marine life, and a good level of scientific information available to help in their management, there can be no better recipe for a park. But not every place that should be conserved has such a profile.

Protecting Biodiversity

In the Southeast Asian tropics, it is known that lowland rain forests harbor the greatest diversity of both plant and animal life. It is also known that, in any given patch of lowland forest, many species are rare. The tall, majestic forests of Borneo contain living spaces for an enormous variety of species. When this tree-enclosed living space is reduced as often occurs, for example, in oil-palm plantations where previously present species have also been systematically removed, we cannot speak anymore of worthwhile biodiversity. The same is true of a reef in its natural state—the coral formations are built on an undisturbed history long enough to establish the complicated architecture that attracts all forms of marine life, enriching the food chain and keeping everything in balance.

Managing our forests carefully to prevent undue degradation or loss should be our central aim. Sustainable forest management cannot be practiced when the amount of timber taken is determined solely by market demand, because high demand can rapidly exhaust the supply of timber stock in a forest, leaving conditions insufficient for proper regrowth. Protecting the forest's ability to sustain basic ecological functions and keep its high biodiversity should be our first priority, followed by the goal of producing a subsequent crop in a reasonable time interval. With such high biodiversity, and with so many rare species scattered in the general lowland forests, we cannot concentrate merely on scenic sites. We must conserve many additional sites, from very large to very small. After all, they are for us, too.

The true value of biodiversity in the rain forests is difficult to define and often impossible to evaluate in monetary

Spider crab on black coral

terms. We need to consider, however, use values connected to human manipulation of the environment. Examples of use value are crop species used in agriculture, the use of wild genes in crop breeding, the tourism value of a forest park, and the ecosystem maintenance provided by a catchment forest. Then, there are nonuse or "existence values," which refer to the value attached by people to the continued existence of a species, such as the rhinoceros (assuming the horns are no longer the target). What seems to be missing in most conservation planning is an emphasis on the fact that the health of an ecosystem (here in the humid tropics) is directly gauged by the species richness it holds. If we think about "damaged" or already destroyed habitats, this is exactly what happens—the biodiversity declines, and we soon lose sight of the original conditions we intended to save. Thus, total habitat destruction or clearance is the most serious form of threat to conservation.

Human actions, such as logging and intensive or degenerative forms of fishing, will affect all of the remaining plant and animal species in a forest or reef system. The severity of the effect depends on how intensive the disturbance has been to the environment. If the level of disturbance is light, many species can be expected to survive, but if it is heavy, or if it is so intense that the basic environment is drastically altered, many more types of plants and animals will experience negative effects or disappear entirely.

"Islands" versus "Fragments"

In the language of conservation, an island is a site with conditions vastly different from those in the surrounding environment; a fragment is some component portion thereof—implied as being minimal and left over, or not particularly planned for retention. Fragments exist within a sea of drastically (and recently) modified conditions; that is, they are left behind in a damaged environment.

Sometimes, conservation of a small patch of forest (referred to as a forest fragment) is not enough to protect the plant and animal species it contains. This is due to what is

Rattan

called the "edge effect," in which species of the modified external environment begin to invade the fringe areas, where conditions are intermediate. Often, these "outside" species are the more common and aggressive species, which successfully compete with the resident species to become better established at the fringe areas. The continuous inward invasion of such species leads to fewer and fewer original species surviving, as the "outside" species take over the forest fragment.

Another thing that can happen is that specialized pollinators of certain plant species no longer thrive in the small forest fragment. In that case, individual plants may persist but will fail to reproduce, and when they die their numbers will decrease, resulting in a gradual loss of the original forest species. Thus, fragments can sometimes be either too small to allow for any viable species conservation or (and this is true, in any case) it will prove impossible to conserve all of the fragment's original

Asian two-horned rhinoceros

species. Despite this fact, because they still may maintain a population of one or two rare or interesting species, the conservation of fragments is better than nothing at all.

For example, it has been estimated that maintaining a viable breeding population of two hundred Asian two-horned rhinoceroses takes at least 1.5 million acres of forest. Maintaining two hundred orangutans requires approximately 38,000 acres. The requirements are different for different species because their life habits and breeding patterns are different. Any real conservation effort must attempt to keep safe an adequate variation in each species being conserved; that is, we must conserve the various genotypes (gene qualities) of each species as much as possible. In the case of rare species, where thousands of acres of forests may house less than a hundred individuals, it will take a lot of study to understand whether this small population is, ultimately, genetically viable;

that is, will it eventually reproduce and maintain itself without outside help.

Some systems badly transected by disturbances, such as logging roads or passages, cannot persist at all. Peat swamp forests are probably like this. As seen in many parts of Southeast Asia, peat swamps that have been logged inevitably become susceptible to weedy growth that tends to take over, preventing regeneration of the original species. Sabah has some truly special peat swamp forests, such as the perupok swamp forest along estuaries of major rivers on Sabah's east coast, as well as the mixed swamp forest in the southwestern corner of the state.

Sarawak, too, has magnificent peat swamp forests, especially along parts of the coastline and in the Baram area to the north. Peat swamp forests may harbor nearly pure and easily harvested stands of timber, but their ecology, once disrupted, cannot be replaced. Peat swamps are natural points in the evolution of the shoreline in relation to river estuaries. They help maintain the integrity of the coastal and riverine regions in times of severe floods, minimizing the threat of erosion by uncontrolled influxes of water. Take them away or degrade them, and suffer the consequences.

Putting Ideas into Practice

We need to find new answers. As currently practiced, extreme forms of conservation such as saving animals in zoos, aquatic life in aquariums, and plants in gardens are but supplementary measures. Often implemented after the destruction is widespread, they are also very expensive to maintain. Many of the plants and animals shown in this book—from the orangutan and *Rafflesia* of the rain forests to the sea turtles and sharks in the reefs—are threatened with extinction, some species due to habitat destruction, some to hunting or poaching and other destructive practices. It is time for us to make a stronger effort to save our heritage and protect the biodiversity of one of the most beautiful regions on Earth. To that end, everyone can take part in conservation, either by contributing to specialized projects such as WWF Malaysia's "Forests for Water, Water for

Life" (FWWL) program or, more generally, by engaging in conservation-related activities—for example, avoiding wasting paper, wood, water, and fuel in the knowledge that these are obtained from natural resources.

In the end, the warning issued not too long ago, in the form of a definition, rings loud: Sustainable development is development that meets the needs of the present without compromising the ability of future generations to meet their own needs. This means that whatever we do should be at a level that will not deplete resources and opportunities for future generations. That is conservation.

Clown anemonefish and porcelain crab in host anemone

Overleaf: Schooling round-faced batfish

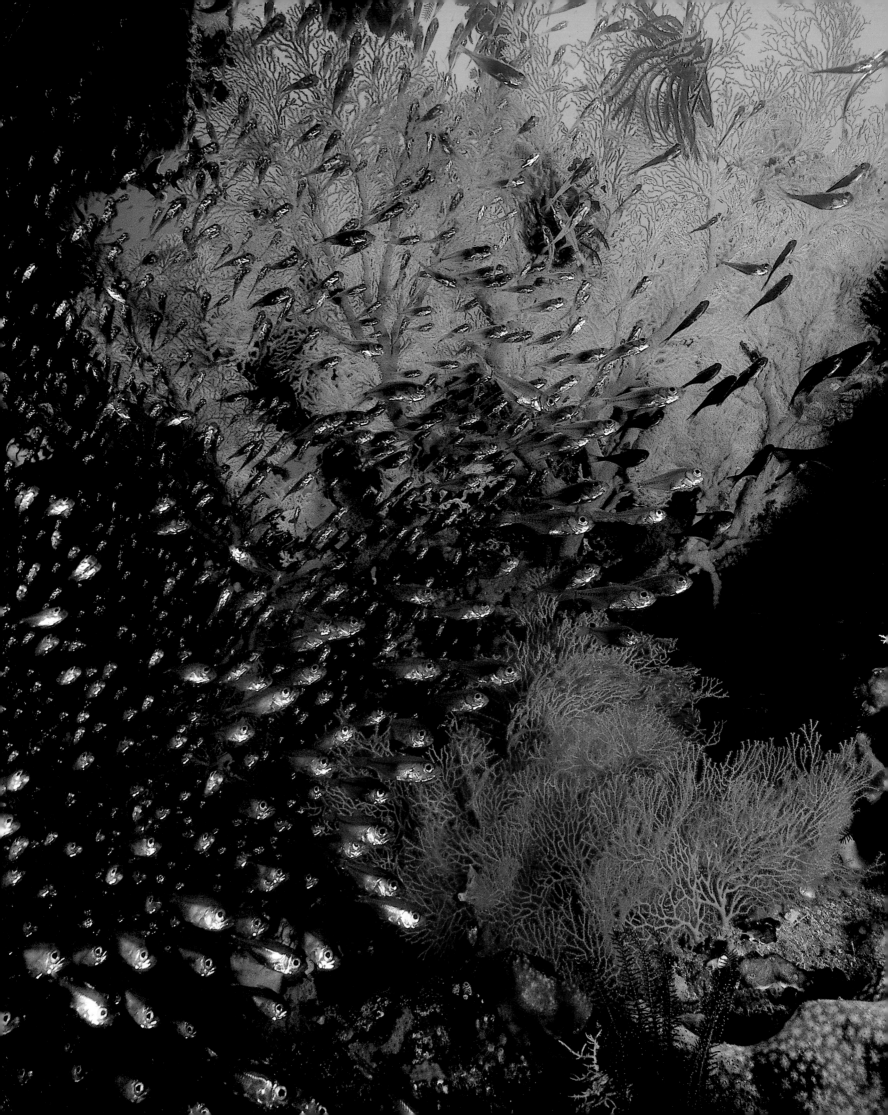

Opposite: Mating bigfin reef squid
Above: Hawksbill turtle

Above: Whitetip reef shark

Opposite: Shoaling barracudas

Above: Green sea turtle

Opposite: Mating green sea turtles

Overleaf: Rain forest scenic

Opposite: Male orangutan

Above: Infant orangutan

Overleaf: Asian two-horned rhinoceros

WWF Malaysia

The World Wildlife Fund (WWF) Malaysia was established as a national charity in 1972, becoming the nineteenth national organization to join the international WWF network. Early work by the WWF focused on helping to establish parks and sanctuaries for wildlife, as well as on nature education. In recent years, WWF Malaysia's goals have expanded, with conservation efforts increasingly focused on environmental protection in the context of total national development.

Today, WWF Malaysia's efforts in the rain forests include the "Partners for Wetlands" program, which works to foster good management of the Kinabatangan River and its neighboring floodplains; and the "Forests for Water, Water for Life"

(FWWL) program, dedicated to preserving Malaysia's water supply through rain forest conservation. In the area of marine conservation, WWF Malaysia's projects include the Semporna Islands Project, the Ma' Daerah Turtle Sanctuary Centre, and creation of a Marine Education and Awareness Centre in Malacca.

In support of their diverse and wide-ranging efforts to protect, conserve, and in some cases restore the beauty and natural biodiversity of the rain forests and reefs for future generations, a portion of the profits from sales of this book will be donated to WWF Malaysia.

Lowland rain forest canopy

Technical Notes

The rain forest and underwater worlds may be the two most difficult environments in which to make photographs, due to the nature of where you are working and the physical and technical demands placed on the photographer. Images made in the rain forest often require long exposures and fill, total, or projected flash. To accomplish this, I use a carbon fiber Gitzo tripod and Nikon flashes powered by rechargeable, rapid recycling Quantum batteries. Flash projection is achieved with a simple fresnel device called a Better Beamer. The heat and humidity of the rain forest exact a heavy toll on cameras and lenses. I began using Nikon N90s camera bodies, which "died" multiple times after moisture contamination. After many costly repair bills, I switched to the Nikon F5 camera, which is nearly indestructible, has wonderful metering and lightning-quick autofocus, which is a joy to use when you need it. More recently, I added a Nikon F100 body to my arsenal for hand-held action shots. Nikon lenses ranging from 20 to 500 mm plus teleconverters and extension tubes were also employed to make these images. Supplemental but essential equipment includes camera plates, brackets, tripod ball and gimbal heads, and flash arms from Really Right Stuff, Arca Swiss, and Wimberly.

Under water, a photographer is faced with even greater obstacles than on land. Some of the images in this book, especially the close-up or macro images, were made with Nikon F4 cameras using a variety of lenses, extension tubes, teleconverters, and diopters. Since the underwater photographer's eye is far from the viewfinder (due to the housing and face mask, which intervene) it is essential, in my opinion, to use a camera, such as the F4, that has a supplemental action finder, which allows full-frame viewing. The F4 cameras are housed in reliable and precision-made Nexus housings. Other images in the book, especially the wide-angle ones, were made with a Nikon RS. This dedicated underwater camera is complemented by excellent water-contact lenses including 13 mm fisheye, 20-35 mm zoom and, more recently, an outstanding 18 mm rectilinear lens custom made by Rene Aumann and distributed by Chris Newbert. Most underwater images are partially or completely lit by strobes. To this end, I use Ikelite 50 strobes for macro photography and Ikelite 200 strobes for wide angle. Both appear to have ideal color temperature and recycle times to be very effective. Probably the most important technical consideration in making underwater images is the watertight seal of the equipment. All photographic equipment must be protected from the dreaded and unspoken "f" word, otherwise known as a flood. To this end, underwater camera equipment is only as good as the seals created by its O-rings, which must be constantly serviced before and after every dive.

In my opinion, film choices are highly subject to personal tastes. Originally, most of my macro photos made above and below water were made with Fuji Velvia. Despite great colors and minimal grain, this slow speed film is often unsuitable for underwater wide-angle or rain forest scenic photography where faster film speeds are essential. Fortunately, during the process of making images for this book, Kodak developed a fantastic line of professional Ektachrome films. My preference for underwater wide-angle films has become E100SW, while my preference for rain forest images is E100VS or E200.

Photo: Lea Eckerling Kaufman

Montane rain forest

Photographer's Notes

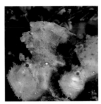

ii–iii

Leaf scorpionfish, Mabul Island, *Taenianotus triacanthus*.

Leaf scorpionfish can be found in a rainbow of colors—yellow, green, brown, black, pink, red, and even silvery-white—depending on the substrate they perch upon. Because leaf scorpionfish have the ability to rapidly distend their mouths, unsuspecting prey that swim by these cryptic ambush predators can be suddenly inhaled.

iv–v

Orangutans, mother and infant, Sepilok Rehabilitation Center, Sandakan area, *Pongo pygmaeus*.

The orangutan is called the "Old Man of the Forest." Thousands have been taken from the rain forest for pets, or they have been driven out because of habitat destruction. At the Sepilok Rehabilitation Center, a successful program has been very effective in helping return orangutans to the forest. This wild mother and young infant, less than three weeks old, appeared unexpectedly. The baby will not let go of the mother, even for a second.

vi–vii

Reef scenic, Barracuda Point, Sipadan Island.

Tropical coral reefs, like those found in the Sulawesi Sea, require warm water and lots of sunlight for development. Coral reefs are often compared to tropical rain forests because of their great ecological complexity and immense diversity of species. The coral reefs of Malaysian Borneo are thought to have the greatest biodiversity of marine species found on Earth.

viii–ix

Rain forest scenic, Danum Valley Conservation Area.

The presence of ancient and massive Dipterocarp trees makes the lowland rain forests of Malaysian Borneo the tallest rain forests in the world. The name "dipterocarp" comes from the Greek for "two-winged fruit or seed," a characteristic of these rarely flowering trees. These enormous trees have huge buttressing roots to support their trunks and their cauliflower-like crowns, which often project more than two hundred feet high to form the dense rain forest canopy.

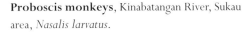

Shoaling barracudas, Sipadan Island, *Sphyraena putnamiae*.

Huge shoals (schools) of barracudas, numbering in the thousands, can be seen predictably at deep-water drop-offs. The shoals continuously change shape, forming patterns, such as dense balls, circles, waterfalls, and tornados. When shoaling, the barracudas are harmless. On many occasions, I have been completely encircled by these awesome fish without any threat of danger.

x–xi

Proboscis monkeys, Kinabatangan River, Sukau area, *Nasalis larvatus*.

There are two types of groups of these unique monkeys, the "harem" and the "bachelor's group." In the harem, there is one huge, dominant male that can be readily identified by his bright red penis, which remains erect when he is challenged by other males for dominance of his females. In the bachelor group, males of different maturation stages are seen together. The prankish behavior of these two bachelors reminds me of my two rival-rous, but mutually-loving, children.

xiii

Green turtle, Sipadan Island, *Chelonia mydas*.

Huge numbers of green and hawksbill turtles gather at Sipadan Island to mate and nest. While these animals are endangered species worldwide, here the large population, which is accustomed to divers, makes close encounters a common occurrence at Sipadan Island. Green turtles are often seen resting on the reef or in caves and undercuts. Hawksbill turtles can sometimes be seen digging and damaging stony corals in their enthusiasm to find delectable sponges to eat.

xiv–xv

Clouded leopard, Tabin Wildlife Reserve, *Neofelis nebulosa*.

The largest cat in Malaysian Borneo, the clouded leopard is a nocturnal animal that is rarely seen and even more rarely photographed. His diet includes pigs, deer, monkeys, small mammals, and even orangutans. This individual was spotted near our blind at the edge of an oil palm plantation where it was thought the cat went nightly to hunt for rats. A long lens, projected flash, lots of patience, and, even more importantly, luck resulted in this image.

xvi

xx

Long-tailed macaque, Kinabatangan River, Sukau area, *Macaca fascicularis*.

These monkeys are also known as crab-eating macaques. They are seen traveling through the canopy in noisy groups of twenty to thirty or more individuals. Unlike other monkeys in Malaysian Borneo, they spend a large proportion of their active time in low trees and scrub, especially along river and mangrove areas. Their diet consists of fruits, as well as a huge array of small animals, including insects, frogs, and crabs.

xxii

Leaf scorpionfish, Mabul Island, *Taenianotus triacanthus*.

When searching for "macrosubjects," a photographer must closely examine the reef for the smallest details. This can be very slow and painstaking, especially in Malaysian Borneo where reefs have multitudinous nooks and crannies filled with a huge diversity of marine life. On one such foray, I accidentally startled this leaf scorpionfish from his camouflaged perch on a brilliant yellow sponge. Fortunately, he came to rest in a position I could quietly advance upon to make this portrait.

xxvi–xxvii

Mabul Island scenic, looking toward Sipadan Island.

Mabul Island is a coralline island surrounded by a barrier reef system. Residing on the island are Bajau fishermen who make their homes on stilts over the water. Mabul Island is becoming known as a mecca for divers who wish to see a plethora of tiny subjects, in contrast to neighboring Sipadan Island, which is home to huge schools of fish, turtles, and sharks.

xxxii

Flamboyant cuttlefish, Semporna area, *Metasepia pfefferi*.

The flamboyant cuttlefish, also known in Asia as the "flower squid," is a small (four inches long), uncommonly seen creature that is recognized by its brilliant color patterns, which include yellow and rose at the tips of its tentacles. This individual was found on a "muck" dive in the mangrove swamps near the coastal town of Semporna. When surprised by my presence, it swam up into the tea-colored water column and began flashing brilliant colors as a signal to warn me off.

8

Gorgonian sea fans and soft coral, Sipadan Island, *Subergorgia mollis* and *Dedronephthya sp*.

This reef scenic is a typical view of the vertical walls of Sipadan Island, an oceanic pinnacle. Gorgonian sea fans, which may reach heights of ten feet, are commonly seen on stony coral outcrops, where they meet ocean currents to filter crops, where they meet ocean currents to filter plankton. Often, crinoids, or feather stars, live on these fans. *Dendronephthya* soft corals have calcific spicules in their bodies and prickly polyps on their branches. When the current is slack, they collapse into a flaccid mass, but when the current picks up, they become erect for filter-feeding.

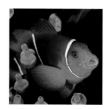
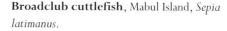

14–15

Spine-cheek anemonefish, Mabul Island, *Premmas biaculeatus*.

This brightly colored clownfish and its host anemone, *Entacmaea quadricolor*, represent the classic example of symbiosis, a term meaning "to live together in nature." Sea anemones, related to corals and more distantly to jellyfish, have nematocysts, or stinging cells, and tentacles to capture and kill prey. Clownfish are protected from these stinging cells by a coating of mucus they get from the anemone. An anemone becomes the territory of the clownfish, which seldom ventures far from it, retreating into its tentacles when threatened.

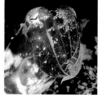

16

Broadclub cuttlefish, Mabul Island, *Sepia latimanus*.

Cuttlefish are not fish, but mollusks in the Cephalopod class, which includes squid, octopus, and chambered nautilus. Cuttlefish have keen vision and can move swiftly, especially if threatened. They readily change color and texture for the purpose of communication and camouflage.

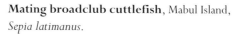

17

Mating broadclub cuttlefish, Mabul Island, *Sepia latimanus*.

I watched with great amazement as this male fought and "beat out" six other males to win the affection of this female. Fortunately, this pair of cuttlefish were oblivious to my close approach as they became actively involved in mating and egg-laying.

18

Squat lobster, Mabul Island, *Lauriea siagiani*.

The body of this elegant squat lobster (one-half inch) is covered with thousands of hairs that are thought to sense movement and to disguise its presence. Only one pair of these animals has been spotted on Mabul Island; they were resting in the folds of a large barrel sponge.

Nudibranch, Kapalai Island, *Flabellina sp.*
Flat worm, Mabul Island, *Pseudobiceros bedfordi.*

Nudibranchs and flatworms are the most spectacularly colored creatures on the tropical coral reef. It is thought that their bright color patterns may warn away predators by signalling toxicity. This nudibranch is laying eggs on its favorite hydroid. Flat worms, like this one, are excellent swimmers when disturbed. They swim by undulating their bodies in rhythmic waves.

19

Needle shrimp in a sea urchin, Kapalai Island, *Stegopontonia commensalis.*

20

The needle shrimp is a very specialized commensal creature that lives on the spines of the black sea urchin, *Diadema*. Just three-quarters of an inch long, its unusual shape helps it to hold on securely to the urchin's spines. Its shape and coloration also provide superb camouflage, concealing it from predators—and photographers!

Porcelain crab in host anemone, Mabul Island, *Neopetrolisthes maculata* in *Heteractis magnifica.*

21

Finning along the reef at dusk, I saw this beautiful anemone with a purple underside in eight feet of water. A spotted porcelain crab was posing perfectly as he extended his seines to filter plankton from the sea. These crabs live in the shelter of sea anemones. They keep from being captured and eaten by the anemone by moving around among the tentacles. They can even enter and leave the mouth of the anemone freely.

Commensal shrimp in hard coral polyps, Mabul Island, *Periclimenes holthuisi.*

22

There are multiple *Periclimenes* shrimp species, most of which are highly transparent. They can be found living within the tentacles of both hard and soft corals. This hard coral, *Goniopora sp.*, has very elongated slender polyps and twenty-four tentacles surrounding a prominent cone-like mouth.

Little file fish, Mabul Island, *Rudarius minutus.*

23

File fish are also known as leather jackets because of their tough, leathery skin. This tiny fish (one inch) is very reclusive; it hides in stalks of soft coral with coloration close to its own. If a predator attempts to eat it, the file fish locks its first dorsal spine into an erect position, stabbing the attacker and forcing its release.

Zebra lionfish, Mabul Island, *Dendrochirus zebra.*

I found this medium-sized lionfish during a night dive on a very shallow reef, and I was struck by the luminosity of its pectoral fins. Lionfish are mostly stationary and reclusive during day and become active at night when they hunt crustaceans and small fish. Their dorsal spines are poisonous; a puncture from one of them can be extremely painful. Even with this risk, which is minimal if you don't provoke the lionfish, the photographic prize is well worth the effort.

24–25

Nudibranch with eggs on stinging hydroids, Ligatan Reef, Semporna area; unidentified, *Doto sp.?*

A nudibranch, or "naked gill," is a sea slug that is found in a variety of shapes and can have strange appendages that make it look like a work of art; it is often referred to as the "orchid of the sea." There are more than a thousand different species, with new ones still being discovered. This individual (one-half inch) was discovered at a depth of 110 feet residing on a small colony of stinging hydroids. It is shown here with its egg case. This remarkable animal is a new species to science.

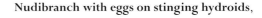

26

Anglerfish with lure extended, Mabul Island, *Antennarius pictus.*

Also known as frogfish, this species has a dorsal fin spine that has evolved into a lure. The anglerfish dangles its lure, which resembles bait—such as a worm or small crustacean—to attract prey. When the victim takes the bait, the anglerfish swallows it whole. This happened so quickly that neither the prey nor this curious photographer saw it coming. This may be the fastest-feeding animal on Earth! Frogfish come in many colors, but this spotted, black-and-gold pattern is rare, which makes this an exciting find.

27

Randall's jawfish, Kapalai Island, *Opisthognathus sp.*

Also called the gold-specs jawfish, this is a relatively new species to science. Jawfish build vertical burrows in open reef patches. They stack rubble and stones around the opening. Jawfish spend most of their time at the entrance, waiting for food to float by. They are very shy and quickly retreat into their burrows when a diver approaches. This is a male, since he is incubating eggs in his mouth. Every so often, he spits the eggs out to aerate them, and then immediately sucks them back into his mouth to continue the incubation. I was thrilled, after many frustrating attempts, to make this image.

28

Adult and juvenile pajama cardinalfish, Mabul Island, *Sphaeramia nematoptera*.

Also known as the coral cardinalfish, this fish lives in groups within the long, complex branches of staghorn corals found at very shallow depths. They are easiest to see around dusk when they come up to the surface of these hard coral formations. This fish species is one of the few known to have both stripes and spots, but how this pattern resembles pajamas remains unclear to me. The adult is three inches long, while the juvenile is less than one-quarter inch in length; this is why the juvenile is rarely seen.

29

Black-rayed shrimp goby, Ligatan Reef, Semporna area, *Stonogobiops nematodes.*

Black sailfin goby, Mabul Island, *Flabelligobius sp.*

Spike-fin goby, Kapalai Island, *Discordipinna griessingeri.*

Rayed shrimp goby, Mabul Island, *Tomiyamichthys sp.*

The four shrimp gobies illustrated here (among dozens of similar species) live in association with blind *Alpheus* shrimp. The shrimp builds and maintains a burrow in which the goby lives. The goby, in turn, guards the entrance to the burrow. Using subtle body language, the goby lets the shrimp know when it is safe to come out. This is a wonderful example of symbiosis or "living together in nature."

Black-rayed gobies are very small (three-fourths inch) and timid, while black sailfin gobies are larger (two inches), but equally shy. Spike-fin gobies (one-half inch) are extremely reclusive and rarely photographed; multiple dives, of nearly two hours each, were necessary to make this image. Rayed shrimp gobies (nearly two inches long) are also usually shy, but this individual made an exception in my case and allowed this portrait to be made.

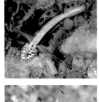

30, 31

Ambonion shrimp, Mabul Island, *Thor amboinensis.*

Holding its tail nearly vertically, this small (three-sixteenths inch) shrimp is seen in pairs or, more commonly, in groups of six to eight. The ambonion shrimp is always associated with anemones or tube worms. In this unusual case, the host anemone was spectacularly colored with purple tentacles and pink spots on its base.

32

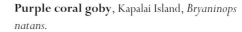

Purple coral goby, Kapalai Island, *Bryaninops natans.*

This tiny reef goby (one-half inch) hovers around or sits atop large, branching hard corals known as *Acropora*. It is easily overlooked since its body is mostly transparent and it blends in with the color of its coral habitat.

33

Golden sweepers, Layang Layang Island, *Parapriacanthus ransonneti.*

These fish are nocturnal, and they disperse at night to feed on plankton. During the day, dense schools of these fish are found in caves. As they turn in unison, they give the impression of a shimmering veil.

34–35

Metallic shrimp goby, Ligitan Reef, Semporna area, *Amblyeleotris latifasciata.*

At first glance, this three-inch-long fish appears to be as drab as the sand and rubble in which it makes its home. Underwater strobe lighting brings out the "metallic" sheen that gives this goby its name.

36

Schultz's pipefish, Mabul Island, *Corythoichthys schultzi.*

Pipefish are related closely to seahorses. Their long, slender bodies are composed of a series of ring-like, bony segments. Like the seahorse, the female pipefish deposits her eggs on the ventral surface of the male, either in a brood pouch or, as in this case, on a specially vascularized surface. The "pregnant" male carries the eggs until they hatch.

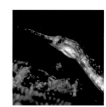

37

Clown anglerfish, Kapalai Island, *Antennarius maculatus.*

Anglerfish or frogfish, as they are commonly called, can be found in a wide variety of colors including white, yellow, pink, orange, red, blue, green, brown, and black. Their color is determined by the substrate on which these ambush predators sit. The distinctive markings of the clown anglerfish are thought to mimic sponges. This is one of the most beautiful fish in Malaysian Borneo.

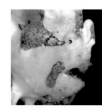

38

Purple fire dartfish, Sipadan Island, *Nemateleotris decora.*

This fish is also known as an elegant fire goby, when, in fact, it is a true dartfish. These shy, small fish (less than three inches long) come out of their burrows to feed on plankton. They are usually seen below seventy-five feet. The purple fire dartfish is easily frightened, and even a slow approach will send it quickly back into its burrow. This particular fish was seen on numerous dives at the entrance to

39

the Turtle Cave at sixty feet and, luckily, since it was preoccupied with feeding, it didn't notice me.

Porcelain crab in a sea pen, Mabul Island, *Porcellanella triloba*.

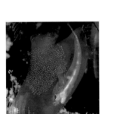

40

Porcelain crabs have modified maxillipeds ("jaw legs") that are covered with long, fine brushes, or seines, used to filter the water for plankton. The food is then passed to their mandibles, or jaws, and ingested. This species of porcelain crab is always associated with a sea pen *(Virgularia sp.)*. In this picture, the female protects her eggs by holding them under her belly.

Cling goby guarding eggs on a tunicate, Mabul Island, *Pleurosicya sp.* on *Rhopalaea sp.*

41

My guide pointed out this female cling goby guarding eggs she had deposited on a simple invertebrate called a tunicate, or sea squirt. The goby was clearly aware of my intrusion but, despite this, she was unwilling to abandon her eggs.

Juvenile cardinalfish in soft coral, Semporna area, *Apogon sp.*

42–43

I was pleased to spot this tiny (three-eighths inch) juvenile cardinalfish hiding within the branches of blue-white soft coral *(Dendronephthya sp.)*. However, it wasn't until I viewed my 35 mm slides that I saw the rainbow of colors glowing from within the fish and was struck with awe.

Bobtail squid, Mabul Island, *Eupyrmna sp.*

The bobtail squid is found in sandy areas in shallow water and is active at night. The squid buries itself in the sand and waits for its prey. It then "jumps" out of the sand and attacks. I surprised this individual and he emerged quickly from his sandy hiding place. He quickly shook off the sand and darted away.

44–45

Arrow crab on octocoral, Kapalai Island, *Eplumra phalangium* on *Carijoa sp.*

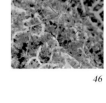

46

I have seen arrow crabs on a variety of sea fans and black corals, but only once on a bright-blue octocoral. The legs of the arrow crab are extremely long and delicate—more than four times the length of its body (one-quarter inch).

Spotted porcelain crabs, Layang Layang Island, *Neopetrolisthes maculata*.

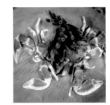

47

At dusk, this anemone closed up, leaving only a few of its tentacles exposed. The crabs crowded together, since they had no place to go for protection. Even though I often see porcelain crabs on sea anemones, I continue to appreciate their beautiful coloration and efficient filter-feeding.

Ribbon eel, Mabul Island, *Rhinomuraena quaesita*.

48

Ribbon eels are found in small sand patches close to coral reefs. They are usually seen with their heads projecting from their holes as they "bob-and-weave" up and down and side to side. Ribbon eels are hermaphrodites and can rapidly change sex and coloration. Juveniles are black with a yellow dorsal stripe. Mature males are bright blue with a yellow dorsal stripe. Mature males transform into females, which are entirely yellow.

Mating mandarinfish, Kapalai Island, *Syndhiropus splendidus*.

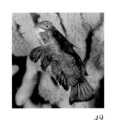

49

Mandarinfish are relatively common in Malaysian Borneo, but are not often seen because of their small size (one-and-one-quarter inch) and their reclusiveness. At dusk, the male comes out and surveys his territory (approximately six square feet). He courts as many as eight females before he selects one for mating. This image was one of the most difficult I have ever attempted, since the timing had to be perfect, and I only got one chance!

Schooling bumphead parrotfish, Sipadan Island, *Bolbometopon muricatum*.

50–51

Bumphead parrotfish are the largest of the parrotfish (up to five feet long). They feed on live corals by biting off huge chunks, digesting the living tissue, and defecating coral sand. Every morning, just before dawn, these parrotfish school at a specific place on the reef. They line up in a formation that resembles a military unit. When the first rays of sunlight appear, they swim off, en masse. This is without a doubt, one of the most incredible underwater sights I have ever seen.

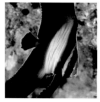

Juvenile pinnate batfish, Mabul Island, *Platax pinnatus.*

This elegant batfish (ten inches) was undergoing transformation from juvenile to adult. It looks nothing like an adult, which is round, silver, and highly reflective. Juvenile pinnate batfish have a distinctive orange outline. They are quite difficult to photograph, since they never stop moving.

52

Picture dragonet, Kapalai Island, *Synchiropus picturatus.*

Only about one inch long, the dragonet is very difficult to spot, and even more difficult to photograph. I have seen only one pair, hidden within shallow soft corals on Kapalai Island. After many frustrating attempts and lots of perseverance, I was rewarded with this image. Note that the body shape is identical to the well-known mandarinfish (see above), but the markings are very different. Nature is incredible!

53

Splendid garden eel, Ligitan Reef, Semporna area, *Gorgasia preclara.*

A small sand patch, less than ten square feet, is the habitat of this remarkably colored, blue-and-gold garden eel. This is the only place I have seen this species. All garden eels are shy, but this one was especially timid and quickly retracted into its burrow when approached. This species was only recently discovered and named.

54

Shrimp in bubble coral, Sipadan Island, *Vir philippinensis.*

After closely inspecting this bubble coral (*Plerogyra sinuosa*) I found these two transparent commensal shrimp, one with eggs inside. Many of my Asian friends think this image is similar to a Chinese painting.

55

Banded sea krait, Kapalai Island, *Laticauda colubrina.*

Sea kraits are marine snakes (reptiles) that come ashore to lay eggs; they don't bear live young. They are venomous, but usually docile, unless aggravated. In my zeal to make this image, I inadvertently trapped this individual, blocking his escape. Suddenly, he became aggressive and "pounced" at my lens. I was shaken, but fortunately unhurt. I had clearly invited this response.

56

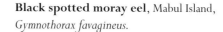

Black spotted moray eel, Mabul Island, *Gymnothorax favagineus.*

Moray eels have elongated, compressed, muscular bodies and very large mouths with multiple rows of very sharp teeth. While morays are capable of inflicting painful wounds, they will not bite unless harassed. When I came upon this moray eel, it was being "groomed" by a white-banded cleaner shrimp, *Lysmata amboinensis.* Cleaner shrimp have an important function—they remove dead scales and parasites from their "customers." For this reason, the eel allows the shrimp to move freely over its body—even inside its mouth and gills—with complete safety.

57

Flamboyant cuttlefish, Kapalai Island, *Metasepia pfefferi.*

This is the most ornate of all cuttlefish. It can alter its colors like a chameleon. When undisturbed, brown-and-white stripes radiate along its dorsum giving the effect of a "barber pole." The flamboyant cuttlefish has modified tentacles that enable it to walk along the reef bottom using a motion that resembles that of a slow-moving elephant. It uses a pair of extensible tentacles to strike its prey.

58, 59

Featherstar clingfish, Sipadan Island, *Discotrema echinophila.*

Clingfish (three-quarter inch) are always associated with crinoids. They have modified pelvic fins that enable them to cling to their host. Clingfish are easy to spot, but difficult to photograph, as they are well-protected by the crinoid's arms.

60

Black wire coral shrimp, Ligitan Reef, Semporna area, *Pontonides sp.?*

Less than one-half inch long, this shrimp was recently discovered on a black wire coral at a depth of 110 feet. Amazingly, this species keeps its eggs on its side. Most experts believe that this is a new species.

61

Scribbled pufferfish eye, Mabul Island, *Arothron mappa.*

About ten different pufferfish are found in the Sulawesi Sea. The scribbled pufferfish can attain a size of twenty-four inches; this one is an intermediate phase between juvenile and adult. These fish are solitary and usually active at night. Pufferfish can inflate themselves into huge balloons—an excellent defense against predators. Also, some pufferfish have a potent neurotoxin in their flesh—eating them as sushi has been fatal in a few cases!

62

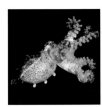

63

Blue ringed octopus, Mabul Island, *Hapalochlaena lunulata*.

A small (two inch), cryptic species, this octopus is distinguished by blue rings that become more intense if the animal is disturbed. This individual, seen on a night dive, swam up into the water column to avoid me. Blue ringed octopuses are known to have a highly toxic bite that can be fatal to humans.

64–65

Thorny sea horse, Kapalai Island, *Hippocampus histrix*.

Sea horses have bodies protected by bony plates and rings, and long tube-like mouths to feed on small crustaceans. They have prehensile tails that wrap around available sponges. The male sea horse has an internal pouch in which he incubates fertilized eggs for several weeks. Finding this creature at sixty feet was a thrilling experience for me.

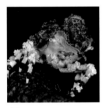

66

Decorator crab, Mabul Island, *Cyclocoeloma tuberculata*.

I found this very handsome decorator crab while on a night dive. This crab (two inches) was covered with corallimorpharians (invertebrates thought to be intermediate between anemones and hard corals), sponges, and tunicates as a means of camouflage. When the crab outgrows its shell and molts, it transfers its adornments or finds new ones to "decorate" its new shell.

67

Decorator crab in colonial coral, Mabul Island, *Achaeus japonicus* in *Euphyllia glabrescens*.

This crab attaches algae to its body for camouflage. It is often found in bubble corals and colonial hard corals, such as this one with unusually long tentacles. Every time I encounter this species, I am reminded of the red, hairy orangutan.

68

Ocellated lionfish, Mabul Island, *Dendrochirus biocellatus*.

This nocturnal hunter is rarely seen during the day. Even at night, it quickly retreats into the caves and crevasses of the coral reef when exposed to bright lights. Like all lionfish, it is a member of the scorpionfish family and, as such, has venomous spines. This spectacular and rarely photographed lionfish has two eye spots which can easily fool predators by making it difficult to distinguish the head of the lionfish from its tail.

Marbled shrimp, Kapalai Island, *Saron marmoratus*.

This shrimp is active at night, but even then remains secretive, hiding in cracks and crevices along the coral reef. This individual is a female as evidenced by the hair on her back, belly, and legs. I have seen this animal only a few times. Fortunately, I had a red filter on my focusing light the evening I made this image. Like most invertebrates, such as crabs and lobsters, this shrimp was unable to see the filtered light, and I was able to make this image.

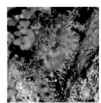

69

Feather duster worm, Mabul Island, *Protula magnifica*.

The head of this polychaete tube worm has evolved into a series of pinnate tentacles arranged in a circular, spiral fashion. The tentacles are used for filter-feeding, as well as for respiration. Feather dusters are found in a rainbow of colors.

70

Squat lobster, Mabul Island, *Galathea balssi*.

Thousands of these squat lobsters (five-eighths inch) can be seen on the sponge-encrusted walls of a deep cave on Mabul Island. This animal was only recently given a scientific name. My dive buddies and I noted its large eyes and named it the "deer-in-the-headlights" squat lobster.

71

Commensal shrimp on a sea pen, Mabul Island, *Dasycaris symbiotes*.

This tiny (one-quarter inch) shrimp lives its entire life on a sea pen *(Pteroeides sp.)*. Sea pens are highly specialized octocorals that are adapted for life in sand or mud. After dusk, the sea pen raises its polyped rachis and catches plankton.

72

Leopard grouper with cleaner shrimp, Mabul Island, *Cephalopholis leopardus* with *Lysmata amboinensis*.

Also known as a rock cod, this beautiful grouper is being "cleaned" of infected skin and parasites by white-banded cleaner shrimp. Surprisingly, the grouper will allow the shrimp to clean its gills and remove food remains from between its teeth. This commensal relationship is one of the truly incredible wonders seen underwater.

73

Decorator crab in soft coral, Mabul Island, *Holophrys oatesii* in *Dendronephthya sp.*

Many different species of crabs use decoration as a means of camouflage, attaching other invertebrates, algae, sponges, tunicates, and corals to their bodies. This soft coral crab not only attaches orange coral polyps for disguise, but it has lines and patterns that mimic the soft coral in which it lives, making it a very private species and a much sought-after photographic subject.

74

75

Flame file shell, Mabul Island, *Lima sp.*

A file shell is a bivalve mollusk closely related to the scallop. This one was discovered deep inside a cave. It flashed neon-like blue waves across its mantle as if it was communicating with me using electrical signals.

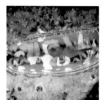

76–77

Variable thorny oyster, Sipadan Island, *Spondylus varians.*

I have seen these huge oysters (ten inches across) a number of times in other places in Southeast Asia, but have never had success in capturing a photograph. The oyster always *saw* me coming (although it probably detected my presence from the pressure wave I created, rather than with its row of blue eyes) and shut rapidly. This specimen, in a cave at forty-five feet, seemed oblivious to me, as well as to the small cave gobies that were walking along its orange-and-blue mantle. Red-and-pink encrusting sponges on its shell completed the kaleidoscopic appearance of this beautiful creature.

78

Octopus, Ligitan Reef, Semporna area, *Octopus cyanea.*

Most octopuses are active at night, but this one is active in the day. It is quite common, but is often overlooked due to its masterful camouflage. It can change colors and textures very rapidly to fool intruders. Octopuses are cephalopods, a class of mollusks. They have eyes that are very similar to vertebrate eyes. They propel themselves by expelling a jet of water through a funnel, as seen in this image. They have glands capable of releasing a black, ink-like substance that confuses predators by creating "false" octopuses. The ink may also anesthetize the chemoreceptive capabilities of some predators.

79

Clown sweetlips, Mabul Island, *Plectorhynchus chaetodonoides.*

This is a juvenile clown sweetlips (four inches). It undergoes a dramatic color transformation as it becomes an adult, gaining an unremarkable coat of dark spots on a light background. This fish is difficult and frustrating to photograph, since it never stops dancing, spinning, and twirling.

80–81

Volitan's lionfish. Layang Layang Island, *Pterois volitans.*

Lionfish are distinguished by having dorsal, anal, and pelvic spines that are venomous. Wounds from the spines vary in intensity from a bee sting to severe agony. Immersion of the injured area in very hot water breaks down the venom and can quickly

relieve the pain. This lionfish was photographed from inside a cave looking outward. It was actively hunting small fish known as cave sweepers.

Emperor angelfish, Sipadan Island, *Pomocanthus imperator.*

Regal angelfish, Sipadan Island, *Pygoplites diacanthus.*

82

Angelfish, close relatives of butterflyfish, are considered to be some of the most beautiful of all reef fish. Seventy-six different species are known from tropical reefs around the world, many of which can be seen in Malaysian Borneo. Living either solitarily or in pairs, angelfish feed on algae, sponges, soft-bodied invertebrates, and fish eggs. The emperor angelfish (fourteen inches) is a large, striking, and often-seen species throughout Southeast Asia. The regal angelfish (eight inches) is very shy and difficult to photograph; the best time is around dusk.

Yellowmask angelfish, Sipadan Island, *Pomocanthus xanthometopon.*

Six-banded angelfish, Sipadan Island, *Pomocanthus sextriatus.*

83

Both of these species are large (sixteen inches), very colorful, and highly visible fish that are usually seen in pairs. While relatively common at Sipadan Island, I have rarely seen these species at other Indo-Pacific locations. Stealth, patience, and a lot of luck resulted in these portraits.

Bigfin reef squid, Mabul Island, *Sepioteuthis lessoniana.*

84

One night, at dusk, I encountered a school of these handsome bigfin reef squid. They can be differentiated from other squid by their lateral fin, which extends down the complete length of the mantle. They are also large (up to one-and-one-half feet) relative to other reef squid. Bigfin reef squid can be very shy. When approached, they will dart away quickly by propelling themselves backward.

Jellyfish with juvenile trevally jacks, Mabul Island, *Crambione mastigophora.*

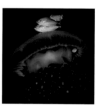

85

Juvenile trevally jacks are sometimes seen swimming with large jellyfish (the bell on this specimen is eight inches). When threatened, the jacks dart under the bell for protection. While the advantages of this arrangement for the jacks is clear, the benefits to the jellyfish remain unknown.

Reef scenics, South China Sea.

I never cease to be amazed by the density of life one can see on healthy, current-swept reefs. In these scenics, one can see a plethora of coral and invertebrate species, including multi-hued *Dendronephthya* soft corals, gorgonion sea fans, *Tubastrea* hard corals, sponges, tunicates, and crinoids. Tropical coral reefs, like these, are the reason why underwater photographers are passionate about saving these delicate and endangered ecosystems from destruction.

86, 87

Schooling trevally jacks, Sipadan Island, *Caranx sexfasciatus*.

Numerous types of fish, including trevally jacks, commonly swim in schools for protection from predators. Jacks hunt individually and alone at night, but frequently return to the same location during the day, forming dense schools, which often resemble rotating rings or balls. On numerous dives at the Dropoff, I had close encounters with these curious fish, even at very shallow depths. This photo was taken at a depth of fifteen feet.

88–89

Strangling fig, Danum Valley Conservation Area, *Ficus benjamina*.

Fig trees are very important as they are a major food source for fruit-eating birds and arboreal mammals. After these animals eat the figs, they drop the seeds on the branches of other trees where they take root. The new fig's root system grows downward, until it anchors in the ground. The fig's roots grow around the host tree trunk and the foliage grows widely through the host tree's crown. Eventually, the fig grows so large that it envelopes the host tree, killing it. In this case, the dead tree rotted away over many years, leaving the fig with its odd, hollow shape.

92

Strangling fig, Danum Valley Conservation Area, *Ficus benjamina*.

I stood within the roots of this strangling fig, where the original host tree had once lived. Looking up nearly two hundred feet into the rain forest canopy was an awesome sight, and it reminded me of being inside one of the great Gothic cathedrals of Europe.

98–99

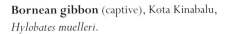

Bornean gibbon (captive), Kota Kinabalu, *Hylobates muelleri*.

Every morning in the Danum Valley Conservation Area, one awakens to the loud, resonant calls of Bornean gibbons. Gibbons are totally arboreal primates which, like other apes, lack a tail. They travel rapidly through the mid- to upper canopy, making photography extremely difficult. They live in family groups consisting of an adult male and female and one to three young. Loss of habitat threatens their existence. This young animal was captured after a forest fire; he will become a resident of a new zoological collection soon to open to the public.

100

Climbing vine, Danum Valley Conservation Area, *Ficus villosa*.

Climbing plants, also known as lianas, are one of the most noticeable features of the tropical rain forest. Climbers, such as this one, grow eagerly upward toward the light, doing little if any harm to adult trees because, unlike parasitic plants, they are merely using their hosts as supports. Old lianas can hang in loops between tree branches or lie in weighty coils on the forest floor. Little is known about the ecology of climbers, but the medicinal value of the many different species of these plants is of great potential interest.

101

Buffy fish-owl, Sukau area, *Ketupa ketupu*.

The buffy fish-owl is primarily nocturnal, but unlike other owls, it can be seen hunting during the day at forest edges and river banks. This large bird is relatively common in lowland rain forests up to three thousand feet. It can be seen bathing or standing in water for long periods of time. Fish, frogs, and crustaceans are the mainstays of the owl's diet.

102

Walker lanternflies, Poring Hot Springs, *Pyrops intricata*.

This is one of the strangest-looking insects of the Malaysian Borneo lowland rain forest. These insects are found on the trunks of Dipterocarp trees, often near the base. Usually I find them singly, but on this occasion I was lucky to see three together. The significance of their color pattern is unknown.

103

Pig-tailed macaques, Sepilok Rehabilitation Center, Sandakan, *Macaca nemestrina*.

Pig-tailed macaques are identified by their distinctive short tails and colorful "eye makeup." They eat just about anything from fruits to small invertebrates, and even small vertebrate animals. At Sepilok, they are wild, but used to man. They

104

105

can be very aggressive if approached too closely. This mother and baby were part of a group of thirty monkeys who were actively trying to break into a restaurant after it closed for the evening. Once bored with this activity, they became focused on feeding and ignored my presence.

106

Rhinoceros hornbill, Sukau Area, *Buceros rhinoceros*.

One of the most spectacular birds of Malaysian Borneo, the rhinoceros hornbill is a regular visitor to fruiting giant strangling figs. These birds have a horny crown, known as a casque, which allows them to make a very loud, harsh "kronk" sound. Also impressive is the dramatic whooshing sound they make when they take off in flight. This female, identified by her white irises, came close to the lodge to eat papaya left for her by the staff.

107

Wreathed hornbill, Danum Valley Conservation Area, *Aceros undulatus*.

This male wreathed hornbill is identified by his creamy head, red irises, and yellow gular (throat) pouch with a distinct black stripe. Wreathed hornbills are fairly common in Malaysian Borneo. They fly in pairs or small flocks over the forest, seeking fruiting trees, where they often mix with other hornbill species. This individual was photographed from a blind more than ninety feet above the forest floor.

108

Green tree lizard, Gomontong Cave area, *Bronchocoela cristatella*.

The green tree lizard is most active in the rain forest canopy where temperatures are very warm (86–92 degrees Farenheit). It can also occasionally be seen in the gardens of homes located on the edge of the forest. This individual was very shy and posed for only two images.

109

Sumatran pit viper, Danum Valley Conservation Area, *Trimeresurus sumatranous*.

Vipers are highly venomous land snakes that possess long, moveable fangs in the front parts of their upper jaws. This viper is arboreal, and it can grow to a length of three feet; this specimen was half that size. Once again, coloration provides excellent camouflage for this deadly predator.

Western tarsier, Danum Valley Conservation Area, *Tarsius bancanus*.

This very small primate (four to five inches) is a solitary animal that can be seen up to twenty feet high, jumping between thin tree trunks. Strictly nocturnal, they hunt and eat grasshoppers and other large insects, which they readily find because of their acute hearing and eyes adapted for night vision.

110

Rajah Brooke's birdwings, Poring Hot Springs, *Troides brookiana albescens*.

There are literally thousands of different butterfly species in Sabah. This resplendent large butterfly, which has a wingspan of up to seven inches, was first discovered by the famous Borneo explorer, Alfred Russel Wallace, in 1855 and named in honor of Sir James Brooke, the Rajah of Sarawak. The Rajah Brooke's birdwing is considered by many to be the most beautiful butterfly in the world. It has become one the symbols of the rain forests of Malaysian Borneo.

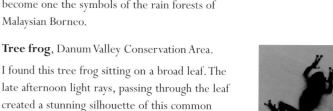

111

Tree frog, Danum Valley Conservation Area.

I found this tree frog sitting on a broad leaf. The late afternoon light rays, passing through the leaf created a stunning silhouette of this common amphibian.

112

Luminous mushrooms, Danum Valley Conservation Area, *Mycena illuminans*. Photo made with Richard McEnery.

It is believed that the light emitted by these fungi, through an oxidation process, attracts beetles and other insects which crawl over the mushrooms. The insects inadvertently gather and scatter mushroom spores across the forest floor. A ninety-minute exposure was necessary to capture the natural luminescence of these remarkable fungi.

113

Western tarsier, Danum Valley Conservation Area, *Tarsius bancanus*.

The tarsier is often described as having the ears of a bat, the eyes of an owl, the fingers of a frog, and the tail of a rat, making it seem to be a creature "designed by a committee." This individual was caught by researchers for brief study, allowing me a rare photo opportunity. It was then released, unharmed, to return to its home territory.

114–115

Giant atlas moth, Danum Valley Conservation Area, *Attacus atlas.*

Seeing this insect is awe-inspiring. This is the largest moth in the world; its wingspan can reach ten inches. This species can be found throughout Malaysian Borneo, from the lowlands to the lower montane elevations. Try to imagine an infestation of these moths in your closet!

116

Giant atlas moth face, Danum Valley Conservation Area, *Attacus atlas.*

A portrait of the face of this incredible giant moth reveals its impressive pectinate (gill-like) antennae. These structures remind me of rhinophores, the sensory organs seen on the heads of nudibranchs (shell-less sea slugs) found throughout the coral reefs of Sabah.

117

Bornean horned frog, Danum Valley Conservation Area, *Megophrys nasuta.*

Even though this frog is widespread in Malaysian Borneo, it is very difficult to find due to its superb camouflage in leaf litter on the forest floor. My guide's trained ear—which allowed him to hear the characteristic "ping" sound this frog makes—coupled with his acute vision, revealed this prize subject to me. The frog stared at me and "winked" his approval with his horned projections when I made myself prone to achieve this "eye level" portrait.

118, 119

Millipede, Danum Valley Conservation Area, *Thyropygus pachyurus.*

Pill millipede, Danum Valley Conservation Area, *Sphaeropoeus sp.?*

Both of these millipedes are invertebrates that live in leaf litter on the forest floor. They forage on fungi and vegetation detritus. The pill millipede (approximately three inches long) rolls into a ball to protect itself against predators.

120, 121

Barking deer, Tabin Wildlife Reserve, *Muntiacus muntjak.*

The barking deer is also known as the red muntjac. This small deer (approximately three feet tall at the shoulder) is known for its loud, distinctive barking calls. This species is active mainly during the day and is usually encountered alone or in male/female pairs. The diet of this beautiful deer includes herbs, young leaves, grasses, and fallen fruits and seeds (including those of Dipterocarp trees).

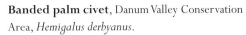

Banded palm civet, Danum Valley Conservation Area, *Hemigalus derbyanus.*

Quite often at night, one sees these omnivorous mammals. There are nine species of civets in Malaysian Borneo. All of them have scent glands that produce a malodorous discharge. Civets are usually seen in forest clearings or on logging roads where they forage for fruits, insects, and small animals, such as birds or lizards. This species lives either in holes in the ground or in trees. This individual was photographed from a blind near some rotting fruit.

123

Sunrise in the Danum Valley, Danum Valley Conservation Area.

This image was made from a fire observation tower near the Danum Valley Field Research Center. I arrived at sunrise to witness the mist rising from the rain forest. When I look upon this scenic image, I think of "islands in the clouds."

124–125

Centipede, Sukau area, *Scutigera sp.*

This long-legged centipede is a very large insect measuring seven inches in length. It has fifteen pairs of elongated legs, plus filamentous antennae. It is commonly seen in caves, such as the Gomontong Cave near Sukau. This specimen, found on a tree trunk, was the only one my guide and I saw during our night treks into the lowland rain forest. The cave species can run very quickly. They feed on bat guano on the cave floor. This is a true "creepy crawler!"

126

Lichen spider, Danum Valley Conservation Area, *Pandercetea sp.*

At night, one can easily spot spiders since their eyes appear pink or red in the light of a flashlight. This large spider, measuring approximately six inches in length, is found on the lichen-covered portion of tree trunks.

127

Red leaf monkey, Danum Valley Conservation Area, *Presbytis rubicunda.*

Also known as the maroon langur, this primate usually lives in groups of eight, one of which is an adult male. Red leaf monkeys feed on young leaves and the seeds of trees and lianas. Their reddish coloration makes them easy to spot, but they are extremely shy and difficult to photograph. After many failed attempts to capture an image, I was having coffee at the lodge when a family group of these monkeys appeared within yards of me! When they saw me, they scampered away; but in their panic, they left behind this bewildered juvenile just long enough for me to get a picture.

128

129

Bracket fungi, Danum Valley Conservation Area, *Ganoderma tropicum.*

Of the many different types of fungi seen in the Malaysian Borneo rain forest, bracket fungi are usually the largest and most prevalent. These fungi grow slowly for years and have a highly polished, waxy crust. My first impression of this specimen was how closely the colors mimicked the striking facial patterns of Bornean gibbons.

130

Male orangutan, Sepilok Rehabilitation Center, *Pongo pygmaeus.*

Male orangutans are twice as big as females; in the wild they can weigh up to 165 pounds. Their arm span is greater than their height, and they can reach nearly seven feet. Males also have luxuriant beards. Adult and adolescent male orangutans always live alone and actively avoid other males. When they do meet, an aggressive confrontation usually occurs. During my numerous visits to Sepilok, only once did I see this wild, sub-adult male. When he appeared, the other orangutans stayed clear of the feeding area.

131

Female orangutan with infant, Sepilok Rehabilitation Center, *Pongo pygmaeus.*

On average, a female orangutan gives birth to one infant every seven to eight years. The infant, weighing approximately three pounds, is born after 245 days (just over eight months) of gestation. The infant clings to its mother for two to three years or more. Once a young orangutan has a new sibling, it starts to separate from its mother and gradually becomes independent. The only close social bond in orangutan society is between adult females and their offspring.

132

Pangolin, Danum Valley Conservation Area, *Manis javanica.*

The pangolin, or scaly anteater, is a distinctive mammal that curls its tail beneath its body when it is disturbed to protect the non-scaly underparts. Usually nocturnal, this pangolin was discovered at dawn. Pangolins open insect nests with their sharp, clawed feet and lick up ants or termites with their long, sticky tongues. This individual was disturbed by my camera flash and "froze" on a broken tree trunk. Serendipitously, a small praying mantis landed on its nose. The photo session was cut short to minimize trauma to this shy animal.

133

Slow loris, Danum Valley Conservation Area, *Nycticebus coucang.*

Nocturnal and usually arboreal, this small primate can only be found at night, its huge eyes reflecting flashlight with a reddish color. The slow loris feeds mostly on insects, small animals, and on pulpy fruits. It is usually solitary. Each time I've spotted this animal, I've wondered if its name is meant to be ironic, since its movements are anything but slow!

134–135

Salt lick, Tabin Wildlife Reserve.

The Tabin Wildlife Reserve, was gazetted in 1984 to protect populations of three endangered large-mammal species: Asian elephants, Asian two-horned rhinoceroses, and Banteng or Asian wild cattle. There are three mud volcanoes where these mammals—along with Sambar deer, bearded pigs, and civets— come to lick the mud which contains necessary minerals. Plans are under way here to build a lodge to promote responsible ecotourism.

136

Asian elephant, Kinabatangan River area, *Elephas maximus.*

The Asian elephant is smaller than its counterpart in Africa. It is estimated that there are only between 500 and 2000 individuals left in Sabah, primarily due to loss of habitat. It is widely accepted that the elephant was introduced to Sabah more than two hundred years ago, but it is also possible, according to some experts, that this mammal may be a native species. This bull was associated with a herd of three adult females and multiple young. On our initial contact he led a charge at me and sent me running. After six hours of stealth (and much trepidation), I was able to get close enough to make this photograph.

137

Binturong, Kinabatangan River area, *Arctictis binturong.*

Also called a bearcat, the binturong is a medium-sized mammal (nearly three feet long and weighing up to twenty pounds) in the civet family. It has a prehensile tail used for balance while feeding in fruiting trees. Also, unlike the other eight civets of Malaysian Borneo, which are silent, the binturong utters low growls and hissing sounds or howls loudly. This animal is primarily nocturnal but, as in this case, can occasionally be spotted during the day.

138–139

Forest scenic, Tabin Wildlife Reserve.

At dusk, the forest takes on a very "magical" and "moody" aura. As daytime creatures find shelter for the night, a very different "cast of characters" prepares for nocturnal hunting and foraging. This is my favorite time to hike quietly on undisturbed trails, listen, and observe.

140

Cinnamon tree frog, Sukau area, *Nyctixalus pictus.*

A small frog (two inches) with a relatively long snout and long hind limbs, the cinnamon tree frog is appropriately named for its handsome coloration. This individual was found "posing" on a small tree trunk approximately three feet above the ground. This is a fairly common species found throughout the rain forests of Malaysian Borneo, from sea level up to 4500 feet.

141

Reticulated python, Danum Valley Conservation Area, *Python reticulatus.*

This snake holds the record as the longest snake in the world, with documented examples of up to thirty feet in length! The reticulated python is one of the more common snakes in Malaysian Borneo lowland rain forests, especially near rivers. While huge ones are rare in Borneo today, it is still not unusual to find them up to twelve feet long. Pythons are well suited to feed on a wide variety of warm-blooded vertebrates using their powerful jaw muscles and long, recurved teeth.

142

Leopard cat, Kinabatangan River near Sukau, *Felis bengalensis.*

The size of a large house cat, the leopard cat is the most common of the five cats in Malaysian Borneo. This cat is primarily nocturnal and terrestrial. Its diet includes small mammals and large insects. This individual was spotted at night along the river's edge, just after a heavy rain. I have also seen many leopard cats along the perimeters of oil palm plantations where they are believed to hunt rats.

143

Masked palm civet, Danum Valley Conservation Area, *Paguma larvata.*

Like other civets in Malaysian Borneo, this species is primarily nocturnal. Unlike its cousins, who are terrestrial, the masked palm civet can also climb trees. It has a highly varied diet including small invertebrates and vertebrates. The civet is a scavenger and is particularly attracted to rotting food—which is how I lured it near enough to make a picture.

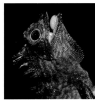

144

Comb-crested agamid lizard, Danum Valley Conservation Area, *Gonocephalus liogaster.*

The lower portion of the rain forest (up to twenty feet) is usually in perpetual twilight. If one looks closely at small tree trunks in this range, one can often spot these large (fourteen inches, head to tail) lizards. Resembling tiny dinosaurs, these creatures remind me how closely the rain forests are connected to their primeval past.

145

Bushy-crested hornbill (captive), Kota Kinabalu, *Anorrhinus galeritus.*

The bushy-crested hornbill is an abundant species found in lowland and sub-montane rain forests. They live in noisy flocks of five to fifteen and feed in the middle canopy, as opposed to other hornbills, which usually feed in the upper canopy. This individual will soon move to her new home in the Kota Kinabalu Zoo.

146–147

Sunrise, Kinabatangan River, near Sukau.

At sunrise, the mist lifts from the mighty Kinabatangan River. Hornbills fly overhead and Bornean gibbons cry out. Traveling along the river at this time of day assaults all the senses at once. Most noticeable is the smell of verdant forest, which recalls the creation of the world.

148

Adult male proboscis monkey, Kinabatangan River, *Nasalis larvatus.*

If another male approaches the territory of a dominant male, the harem leader gives a spectacular display of strength. He begins by leaning forward on all fours with his chin thrust forward and his mouth wide open. Then he suddenly leaps through the trees with a loud roar. Frequently, he lands on dead branches, which break with a loud crack. Chases are common, but actual contact between rival males is rare. Occasionally, an intruder falls into the river. His webbed feet help him swim quickly to avoid crocodiles.

149

Female proboscis monkey with infant, Kinabatangan River, *Nasalis larvatus.*

Compared to that of other monkeys, social life inside a proboscis harem is pretty quiet. Blue-black faced infants are groomed by their mothers, while juveniles play with each other. Grooming or any interaction between adults—besides mating—is rare. The female, much smaller than the male, sometimes initiates mating by presenting her backside and leaning forward on all fours. Turning her head to face the male, she wags her head from side to side and pouts her lips. The male seems to find this irresistible!

150

Black and red broadbills, Menanggol River, *Cymbirhynchus macrorhynchus.*

Early in the morning, after the mist rises from the river, is the best time to see a plethora of birdlife. Broadbills, kingfishers, trogons, paradise flycatchers, pittas, bee-eaters, and oriental darters are but a few of the many commonly seen bird species. Broadbills often build their nests on dead tree snags in the middle of rivers.

151

Riverine rain forest scenic, Menanggol River.

Sunrise is a peaceful time on this tributary of the Kinabatangan River. This is an ideal time to see groups of proboscis monkeys as they begin their morning foraging. Usually, you can smell their strong, pungent odor before you see them. My guide calls this tree the "jumping" tree, since proboscis monkeys often use it to cross the river.

152

Blue-eared kingfisher, Menanggol River, *Alcedo meninting*.

Often, I have seen these birds perched on small branches just above the river. The kingfisher makes lightning fast dives into the water to catch its prey, which it kills and eats on the perch. This individual was photographed at night.

153

Stork-billed kingfisher, Menanggol River, *Pelargopsis capensis*.

This spectacular bird is the largest of the kingfishers in Borneo, measuring nearly fourteen inches in length. It lives in pairs, but hunts alone, making spectacular dives. When disturbed, it flies fast and low, skimming the water like a streak of turquoise neon—a truly incredible sight.

Horned spiders, Sukau area, *Gasteracantha arcuata*.

Originally, I thought that these two spiders were the same species with a variation in color. Entomologists believe that they are probably different species, and that the yellow one may be a new species to science! There are millions of different insects in Malaysian Borneo, possibly more than anywhere else on the planet. Taxonomy of this massive class of invertebrates is unresolved and will need further study.

154

155

Dillenia **flowers**, Segama River, Danum Valley Conservation Area, *Dillenia excelsa*.

Towering *Dillenia* trees, growing up to one hundred feet tall, are common along river banks in lowland rain forests. They produce these spectacular, large (six-inch) flowers. The flowers bloom in the morning and die by evening, dropping their petals into the rivers and streams. They provide a food source not only for birds, but also for fishes.

Juvenile purple herons, Likas Wetlands, Kota Kinabalu, *Ardea purpurea*.

Likas Wetlands is a new sanctuary created within Sabah's bustling capital city of Kota Kinabalu. Purple herons have begun to nest here in large numbers. These juveniles were photographed while they were "croaking" at each other. It reminded me of when my children were young and at play.

156

Stick insect, Sukau area, *Haaniella echinata*.

I found this stick insect on a night trek through the forest. While there are many varieties of stick insects in Malaysian Borneo, this is one of the few spiny ones. It grows to six inches long. When threatened by a predator, it rubs its wing covers violently against its lower wings to produce a hissing sound. This stick insect lays the largest eggs known in the insect world, up to three-eighths of an inch long! If you look closely at this image, there is a one-inch-long juvenile near the head of its mother.

157

Forest scenic, Poring Hot Springs area, *Amorphophallus sp.*

Walking along a quiet trail, I came upon this rare flower, known only as a member of the *Amorphophallus* genus. Little is known about this strange, prehistoric-looking inflorescence, which is eighteen inches in height and twelve inches in diameter. This rare find is an example of the many wonders still awaiting the adventurous explorer in Malaysian Borneo's rain forests.

158–159

Rafflesia **buds**, Poring Hot Springs area, *Rafflesia keithii*.

Rafflesia are parasitic plants that penetrate a wild forest vine called *Tetrastigma*. How *Rafflesia* seeds germinate within the *Tetrastigma* vine is unknown, but after one-and-a-half years, a bud appears. It takes up to nine months for the bud to mature and bloom. Most buds rot in excessive rains, shrivel up during drought, or are eaten. *Rafflesia* produces only a single flower. The plant has no leaves, stems, or roots. At this writing, it has never been successfully transplanted or cultivated.

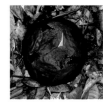

160a

Rafflesia **flower**, Mamut Rafflesia Sanctuary, Ranau, *Rafflesia keithii*.

This *Rafflesia* flower is the largest of the three seen in Sabah, measuring up to three feet in diameter! Like all *Rafflesia*, this flower emits a mildly foul odor that smells like rotting meat. This is thought to attract carrion flies that may cross pollinate male and female flowers (however, since both male and female flowers need to be blooming in proximity,

160b

this theory is questionable). How the seeds are dispersed is also unknown—perhaps by wild pigs, ground squirrels, tree shrews, ants, termites, or elephants, which eat the flowers.

161a

Rafflesia flower, Rafflesia Sanctuary Forest Reserve, Crocker Range, *Rafflesia pricei*.

Rafflesia flowers feel rubbery and artificial. Blooms last only three days, then die. The flower of *Rafflesia pricei* grows to a diameter of ten to fifteen inches. It has conspicuous, large white warts on its perigone lobes, which readily distinguishes it from other *Rafflesia*. Mysterious biology, highly restricted habitats, and very short lifespan make *Rafflesia* flowers extremely rare. This species is monitored at the Reserve and is probably the most accessible.

161b

Rafflesia flower, eastern slopes of Mount Trus Madi (and also recently seen in the Maliau Basin), *Rafflesia tengku-adlinii*. Photograph courtesy of Tengku Datuk Dr. Zainal Adlin.

A third species—the smallest (five to six inches) and rarest of Sabah's *Rafflesia*—*Rafflesia tengku-adlinii*, was discovered in 1987. It was named for Tengku Datuk Dr. Zainal Adlin, the renowned conservationist, and author of this book's conservation chapter. *Rafflesia* may be a link to our prehistoric past. Its ethereal nature makes it a perfect symbol for the delicacy of the rain forest.

162

Malay lacewing, Poring Hot Springs, *Cethosia hypsea hypsina*.

One of the most stunning of the thousands of species of butterflies in Sabah, this species emits a foul odor if touched. The pattern and colors of this butterfly remind me of a rare and valuable oriental carpet.

163

Praying mantis, Poring Hot Springs, Order Mantodea.

Praying mantises have the ability to turn their heads and look over their shoulders with their bulging compound eyes. These insects are carnivorous. They slowly stalk their prey until they are close enough to swiftly grab the victim with their front legs. This small, colorful mantis (less than one-half inch) reminds me of similar-looking shrimp foraging on the reef at night.

Aerial view, summit of Mount Kinabalu. Photo courtesy of Tengku Datuk Dr. Zainal Adlin.

The granite massif, Mount Kinabalu, rises to 13,455 feet. It is the highest peak between the Himalayas and New Guinea. Its phenomenal biological diversity, possibly the greatest on Earth, has

164–165

captivated scientists since it was first climbed by Hugh Low in 1851. Even today, Kinabalu has not been fully explored. After establishment of the Kinabalu Park in 1964, careful conservation efforts have been made to minimize human impact on this delicate ecosystem, while still allowing tourists the opportunity to experience much of the mountain.

Kinabalu balsam, Mount Kinabalu, *Balsaminacea sp.*

This impatiens, or balsam flower, is common along the summit trail of Mount Kinabalu, beginning at around 6000 feet. It grows in the moist, damp understory near streams and waterfalls. At this time, a formal botanical description has not been published.

166

Lobelia, Mount Kinabalu, *Lobelia borneensis*.

One can be easily fooled into thinking that lobelia are orchids. These purple-violet blooms are a common sight at Mesilau, on the east side of the mountain. Mount Kinabalu is a paradise for those who love flowering plants.

167

Rothschild's slipper orchid, Mount Kinabalu, *Paphiopedilum rothschildianum*.

Of all the orchids in the world, this is one of the most sought-after by collectors. The few known populations of this species, which is indigenous to Mount Kinabalu, are endangered in part due to natural catastrophes, such as fires, and in part due to plant thieves. Because of its rarity, this slipper orchid is referred to as "Kinabalu Gold."

168

Orchid, Mount Kinabalu, *Pantlingia lamrii*.

On a trail in the mossy rain forest, my guide showed me this tiny orchid (less than three-sixteenths of an inch) growing only one inch above the soil. On my knees, I photographed this remarkable flower at high magnification (3x). After the film was examined by experts, I learned that this is a new species. It was unclassified at the time this image was made. Only recently was it given its scientific name. Mount Kinabalu is truly Borneo's magic mountain!

169

Pitcher plant, Mount Kinabalu, *Nepenthes burbidgeae*.

Pitcher plants are probably the most bizarre plants in the world. They are carnivorous, producing jug-shaped leaf extensions that have evolved to attract, trap, and digest animals for nutritional benefit. The products of digestion are absorbed through the walls of the pitcher and transported throughout the plant to provide energy for growth and reproduction. Of the nine species found on the

170

slopes of Mount Kinabalu, *Nepenthes burbidgeae* is the least common.

171

Pitcher plant, Mount Kinabalu, *Nepenthes villosa*.

We had to hike the steep and demanding summit trail on Mount Kinabalu to the upper slopes at 9,500 feet to see this spectacular pitcher plant. *Nepenthes villosa* grows at higher altitudes than any other *Nepenthes* in Borneo. It is found in the mossy forest where the air is saturated by clouds for much of the day. Seeing this unusual pink, red, and yellow specimen was well worth the grueling trek.

172

Pitcher plant, Mount Kinabalu, Mesilau area, *Nepenthes rajah*.

The huge *Nepenthes rajah* (twelve to fifteen inches long) is without a doubt the most famous of the pitcher plants. The pitcher—which can hold up to three quarts of liquid—has been known to trap insects, as well as rats, frogs, and lizards!

173

Trilobite beetle, Mount Kinabalu, *Duliticola sp.*

If you walk the trails near the park headquarters of Mount Kinabalu, you will surely see this two-inch-long beetle on the moist forest floor, feeding on rotting wood. The trilobite beetle is appropriately named as it looks like the extinct, ancient trilobite. In fact, some fossils so closely resemble this beetle that certain experts consider the trilobite beetle to be a living prehistoric species.

174–175

Medinella, Mount Kinabalu, *Medinella speciosa*.

Medinella is a common shrub seen around the park headquarters of Mount Kinabalu. This is one of the seventeen *Medinella* species known from the mountain; there are forty-eight species throughout Borneo. Early morning dew enhances the subtle shades of pink, red, and purple found in these resplendent berries.

178

Aerial walkway, Danum Valley Conservation Area.

Early in the morning, as the mist lifts from the Danum Valley, this walkway is a wonderful place for scientists and visitors to study the canopy, one-hundred-fifty feet above the forest floor. Protection of this critically endangered habitat has been ensured by the Sabah Foundation, an organization that manages this conservation area. Among their strategies for sustainable development is a plan to allow only a very small number of tourists and tourism operators access to this special place.

Schooling round-faced batfish, Sipadan Island, *Platax teira*.

Among the most graceful of coral reef fish, batfish are very tame and easily approached by divers. This school swarmed around me at Barracuda Point. The destruction of shallow, fringing coral reefs by dynamite fishing, careless dropping of boat anchors, and unchecked pollution create a cascade effect on this delicate ecosystem. In very short order, stunning reef fishes like these will disappear.

184–185

Reef scenic, Layang Layang Island.

Magnificent coral reefs throughout the equatorial tropics are highly threatened by siltation (run-off of top soil after rain forest destruction), waste dumping, pollution, and industrial waste run-off. Cyanide poisoning and dynamite bombing for fish collection, both illegal activities, go unchecked throughout a large part of the tropics. These latter activities, for example, have nearly destroyed the Philippine reef system, one of the greatest in the world. Malaysia is taking positive steps to prevent these destructive activities and preserve her coral reefs.

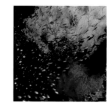

186

Tozeuma shrimp, Kapalai Island, *Tozeuma sp.*

This beautiful shrimp (two-inches) is seen clutching her eggs. New to science, it does not yet have a species name. Undamaged coral reefs harbor many small and unusual creatures, including some that remain undiscovered. Clearly, the health of an ecosystem, such as a coral reef, can be measured in terms of the species richness, or biodiversity, it contains. Preserving biodiversity is, without doubt, one of the most important aspects of conservation.

187

Mating bigfin reef squid, Mabul Island, *Sepioteuthis lessoniana*.

Watching twenty bigfin reef squid mating and then laying eggs into an artificially created environment (a collection of dead palm fronds) is one of the most magical experiences I have experienced in nature. This is an excellent example of how marine life flourishes in clear waters free from siltation and other forms of pollution.

188

Hawksbill turtle, Sipadan Island, *Eretmochelys imbricata*.

Usually, hawksbill turtles ignore divers at Sipadan Island, which is undoubtedly the mecca for turtle encounters in the world. This animal was seen resting inside a huge barrel sponge. This casual interaction between two unrelated species should remind us that the interrelationships of all living creatures in an ecosystem are highly complex

189

and not well understood. What is known is that destruction of any strata of the complex reef ecosystem has a severe, deleterious effect up and down the food chain.

190

Whitetip reef shark, Layang Layang Island, *Triaenodon obesus.*

The whitetip reef shark is one of the most common sharks on the coral reef. It likes to "sleep" or lie on the bottom in caves or, occasionally, in the open. It is a medium-sized shark, found up to six feet in length. It is considered harmless to divers; when disturbed, it will slowly swim away. As apex predators, sharks play a critical role in the oceans. Tragically, they are being destroyed for many reasons including fear, sport, and even greed.

191

Shoaling barracudas, Sipadan Island, *Sphyraena putnamiae.*

Today, marine ecosystems throughout the world are severely threatened by the destructive practice of overfishing. Depletion of huge schools of pelagic fishes will have unpredictable deleterious effects on the ecological balance of marine habitats.

192

Green sea turtle, Sipadan Island, *Chelonia mydas.*

Green sea turtles can reach massive sizes of up to 5 feet long and 350 pounds. They have been hunted throughout the world for their shells, meat, and eggs. They are relatively common in Malaysian Borneo, where they are protected; however, in the rest of the world, they are listed in the IUCN Red List of Threatened Animals as "endangered." Every effort must be made to protect and preserve these ancient mariners of the seas.

193

Mating green sea turtles, Sipadan Island, *Chelonia mydas.*

A receptive female attracts every male in the area. In their fervor to mate, the males climb on top of each other's backs. This "stacking" behavior leaves the female on the bottom, struggling to periodically come to the surface for air. This turtle "orgy" is one of the most amazing sights I have ever witnessed. Ultimately, one suitor wins out, and the male and female begin mating for several hours. At night, the female lays her fertilized eggs on the shore in the same place where she herself was born.

194–195

Rain forest scenic, Segama River, Danum Valley Conservation Area.

Early in the morning, the moisture trapped in the rain forest lifts as a mist, revealing an incredible vista accentuated by the gently flowing Segama River and thousands of ancient Dipterocarp trees. Habitats, such as this virgin lowland rain forest,

are threatened by destruction through human activities and population growth. An effective way to preserve special places, such as the Danum Valley Conservation Area, is to gazette these sites as wildlife sanctuaries.

196

Dipterocarp and seedling, Danum Valley Conservation Area.

In the lowland rain forests of Malaysian Borneo, massive Dipterocarp trees rise to heights of nearly two hundred feet. Huge buttress roots are necessary to support these gigantic trees in the shallow rain forest soil. Dipterocarp roots and soil fungi form symbiotic structures known as mycorrhizas, which provide nutrients to seedlings so they can grow in the absence of sunlight.

197

Rafflesia keithii, Mamut Rafflesia Sanctuary, Ranau.

This astonishing flower is a reminder of the critical need to conserve the vulnerable ecosystem of the rain forest. The same uncontrolled logging, over-development, and pollution that threaten *Rafflesia* with extinction, may result in the destruction of tropical rain forests all over the world.

198–199

Maliau waterfall, Maliau Basin Conservation Area.

Maliau Basin is one of the last unexplored, truly wild places left on Earth. Less than one hundred individuals (primarily research scientists) have taken the arduous trek into this area, called the "Lost World" by the Malaysians. The most recognizable feature of this remote place is a seven-tiered waterfall. More importantly, many new species of plants and animals have been recorded from this unique habitat—and many others remain to be found.

200

Male orangutan, Sepilok Rehabilitation Center, *Pongo pygmaeus.*

This wild, sub-adult male is estimated to be eighteen years old, but he is not yet sexually mature. Like all male orangutans, he is solitary. This is probably due to the fact that he needs a great amount of food to eat and must forage alone over large areas to satisfy this need. Late sexual maturation and solitary behavior are two of the many reasons that orangutans are the slowest of all primates to reproduce. Add hunting and loss of habitat to the equation, and one can readily understand why orangutans are one of the most highly endangered creatures on Earth.

201

Infant orangutan, Sepilok Rehabilitation Center, *Pongo pygmaeus.*

This infant was born to a rehabilitated female, who was impregnated in the wild. This is truly a testament to the incredible and vital work being performed at the Sepilok Rehabilitation Center. Because of the importance of what this image represents, it is, without a doubt, one of my favorites.

202–203

Asian two-horned rhinoceros (captive), Sepilok Rehabilitation Center, *Dicerorhinus sumatrensis.*

This magnificent animal has been hunted nearly to the point of extinction. Once widespread in Southeast Asia, it is estimated that there are only thirty of these animals left in Malaysian Borneo. At Sepilok, veternarians and staff are actively pursuing a captive breeding program. There is a real fear that this animal could become extinct in our lifetime.

204–205

Adult male orangutan, Danum Valley Conservation Area, *Pongo pygmaeus.*

A rare chance encounter brought me less than thirty feet from this "Old Man of the Forest." From the moment we made eye contact, I realized he was as aware of me as I of him. Clearly, the differences between us were too small to discern. Encounters like this one made me aware that we have a duty to ensure the survival of one of our closest primate relatives.

208

Montane rain forest, Mount Kinabalu.

With a dazzling array of flora and fauna, Mount Kinabalu, the highest mountain in Southeast Asia, has drawn huge attention from naturalists, conservationists, climbers, and tourists in general. Four distinct ecological zones—with different associated plants and animals—can be correlated with different altitudes. This clear forest stream passes through a montane rain forest at 4500 feet, where temperatures are refreshingly cool.

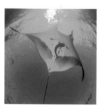

227

Giant manta ray, Layang Layang Island, *Manta birostris.*

The giant manta is one of the largest and most spectacular fish in the tropical oceans of the world. It can measure up to twenty feet from wing-tip to wing-tip. This specimen has a remora or suckerfish attached to its underside. The giant manta is a harmless plankton feeder. When it is feeding, it makes graceful loops and turns, which have been frequently described as the "manta ballet." It is my sincere hope that it is not too late for our conservation efforts to ensure the survival of this magnificent creature and others like it.

Kota Kinabalu, Sabah, Malaysia.

At dusk on a clear evening, Mount Kinabalu can be seen as a backdrop to Kota Kinabalu, the capital of Sabah. All Sabahans, even those residing in this modern city, are acutely aware of the wonders that surround them and their natural heritage is a source of great pride.

228–229

A NOTE ABOUT SCIENTIFIC ACCURACY

Scientific taxonomy—the process by which new species are described, named, and classified—is an ever-changing science, with new species being discovered every day. Although I have some experience in field biology, I'm neither a research scientist nor a taxonomist, either of whom might easily find mistakes I've made in species identification or in my use of terminology, especially in Latin. For that reason, and with all due respect to the experts, any textual errors in the book are unintentional and completely my own.

Opposite: Giant manta ray

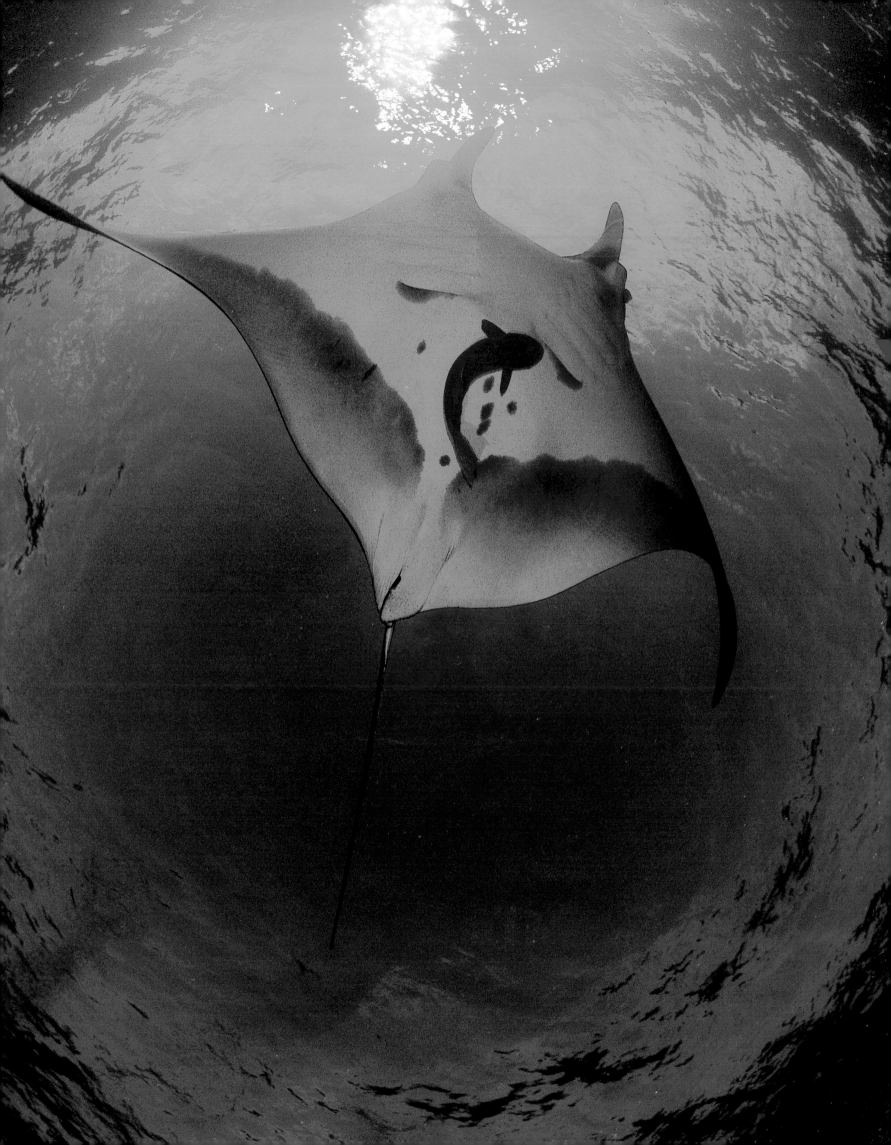

Sponsors

TOURISM MALAYSIA
Malaysia Tourism Promotion Board
Ministry of Culture, Arts and Tourism Malaysia

Our objective is to promote Malaysia as an outstanding tourist destination. Through our activities, we attract the world's attention to the splendor and beauty that is uniquely Malaysian. In turn, the growth of Malaysian tourism will contribute positively to economic development and enhance the quality of life for all Malaysians.

–Tourism Malaysia, www.tourism.gov.my

Malaysia Tourism Promotion Board–Head Office
17th Floor, Menara Dato' Onn
Putra World Trade Centre
45, Jalan Tun Ismail
50480 Kuala Lumpur
Tel: 03.2693.5188
Fax: 03.2693.5884.03
Email: tourism@tourism.gov.my
http://www.tourism.gov.my

Malaysia Tourism Promotion Board–Los Angeles Office
Suite 970, 9th Floor
818 West Seventh Street
Los Angeles, CA 90017
Tel : 213.689.9702
Fax: 213.689.1530
Email: mtpb.la@tourism.gov.my
http://www.tourismmalaysia.com

Malaysia Tourism Promotion Board–New York Office
120 East 56th Street, Suite 810
New York, NY 10022
Tel: 212.754.1113
Fax: 212.754.1116
Email:mtpb.ny@tourism.gov.my
http://www.visitmalaysia.com

Malaysia Tourism Promotion Board–Vancouver Office
830 Burrard Street
Vancouver, British Columbia
CANADA V6Z 2K4
Tel: 604.689.8899
Fax: 604.689.8804
Email: mtpb.vancouver@tourism.gov.my
http://www.tourism-malaysia.ca

Proboscis monkey

Black hornbill

Leaf insect

Dragon

Sponsor

SABAH TOURISM PROMOTION CORPORATION
Ministry of Tourism Development, Environment,
Science and Technology. Sabah, Malaysia

Sabah, Malaysian Borneo, is a treasure trove of natural wonders. Climb to the summit of Mount Kinabalu, the highest mountain in Southeast Asia. Play with the orangutan in a world-renowned sanctuary. Admire the *Rafflesia*, the largest flower in the world, found in the oldest rain forests on Earth. Dive into the planet's most diverse underwater wonderlands. Share in the colorful festivals and ancient traditions of our warm, friendly people. We invite you to discover Sabah.
   —STPC, www.sabahtourism.com

Sabah Tourism Promotion Corporation

51 Jalan Gaya

88000 Kota Kinabalu

Sabah, Malaysia

Tel: 6088.212121

Fax: 6088.212075

Email: info@sabahtourism.com

Ministry of Tourism Development, Environment, Science and Technology

Menara Sabah Bank

Tingkat 5, 6 dan 7

Wisma Tun Fuad Stephens

Karamunsing

88300 Kota Kinabalu

Sabah, Malaysia

White-bellied sea-eagle

Saturn moth

INNOPRISE CORPORATION SDN BHD
Yayasan Sabah (Sabah Foundation)

Yayasan Sabah, or the Sabah Foundation, was established by the state government in 1966, charged with a mission to improve the quality of life of the people of Sabah, particularly in the fields of education, welfare and health. Innoprise Corporation is the investment arm of Yayasan Sabah and the holding and management company for diverse business interests including timber, shipping, real estate, hotels, and tourism. Innoprise Corporation is "acutely aware of its environmental responsibilities to future generations" and, therefore, it strives to manage its forest lands in an integrated and sustainable manner. Hence, "we combine harvesting with major programs of natural forest silviculture, replanting, research, conservation education, and natural history tourism." Reflecting its commitment to sound rain forest management, ICSB has voluntarily set aside two large tracts of undisturbed forest within the Yayasan Sabah Concession Area, the Danum Valley Conservation Area, and the Maliau Basin Conservation Area. ICSB manages the Danum Valley Field Center, a world-renowned research center, and the Borneo Rainforest Lodge, an exclusive facility for natural history tourism.

Innoprise Corporation Sdn Bhd
Corporate Communications Department
15th Floor, Yayasan Sabah Building
P. O. Box 11623
88817 Kota Kinabalu
Sabah, Malaysia
Tel: 6088.426348
Fax: 6088.421254
Email: ysinfo@ysnet.org.my
http://www.ysnet.org.my

Borneo Rainforest Lodge
Block 3, Ground Floor, MDLD 3285
Fajar Centre, P. O. Box 61174
91120 Lahad Datu
Sabah, Malaysia
Tel: 6088.709107
Fax: 6088.709105

Monitor lizard

Slipper orchid

Lesser adjutant stork

Sponsor

MALAYSIA AIRLINES

Over the past 50 years, Malaysia Airlines has grown to become Southeast Asia's largest airline and one of the world's premier international carriers. Flying the most technologically advanced jetliners in the sky, our vast global network serves over 110 cities across 6 continents. We invite you to fly with us and experience the genuine warmth and hospitality that has made Malaysia Airlines a favorite among travelers around the world.

–Malaysia Airlines, www.malaysiaairlines.com

Kuala Lumpur (Home Office)
Bangunan MAS
Jalan Sultan Ismail
50250 Kuala Lumpur, Malaysia, 50716
Tel 6.03.7463000
Fax 6.03.78467733

Los Angeles (North American Headquarters)
100 N. Sepulveda Blvd., Suite 400
El Segundo, CA 90245
Tel 310.535.9288
Fax 310.535.9088
LA Sales-laxsales@malaysiaairlines.com
Reservations-reservations@malaysiaairlines.com

New York
2 Grand Central Tower
140 E. 45th St., 42nd Floor
New York, NY 10017
Tel: 212.697.8994
Fax: 212.867.0325
nycsales@malaysiaairlines.com

Vancouver
885 W. Georgia St., Suite 919
Vancouver, B.C. Canada V6C 3E8
Tel: 604.681.7741
Fax: 604.662.7741
vancouver@malaysiaairlines.com

File-eared tree frog

Jack-in-the-pulpit

Greater mouse deer

Contributor

 SABAH AIR

Sabah Air

Sabah Air
Penerbangan Sabah Sdn Bhd
Sabah Air Building, Old Airport Road
Locked Bag 113,
88999 Kota Kinabalu
Sabah, Malaysia
Tel: 6088.256733
Fax: 6088.235195
Email: enquiry@sabahair.com.my
http://www.sabahair.com.my

With its fleet of helicopter and fixed wing aircraft, Sabah Air provides multiple services, including passenger and cargo transport, aerial filming, survey and mapping, search and rescue, Flying Doctor Service and aerial sightseeing.
        –Sabah Air, www.sabahair.com

Contributor

 TABIN WILDLIFE

Tabin Wildlife Sdn Bhd
Office No. 7, Airport Terminal 2
Old Airport Road, Tanjung Aru
Locked Bag 113
88999 Kota Kinabalu
Sabah, Malaysia
Tel: 6088.264071
Fax: 6088.249158
Email: enquiry@tabinwildlife.com.my
http://www.tabinwildlife.com.my

Owner/operators of a jungle lodge dedicated to wildlife viewing in the largest wildlife reserve in Sabah, Malaysian Borneo.

Bamboo orchid   Helmet orchid   Oriental whip snake   Dragonfly

SUTERA HARBOUR RESORT AND HOTELS

Sutera Harbour Resort and Hotels
1 Sutera Harbour Boulevard, Sutera Harbour
88100 Kota Kinabalu
Sabah, Malaysia
Tel: 6088.318888
Fax: 6088.317777
Email: reservations@suterah.po.my
http://www.suteraharbour.com

Nestled between the shores of the South China Sea, fronting the tropical islands and the majestic Mount Kinabalu, is the grand expanse of Sutera Harbour Resort. The 384-acre resort provides a spectacular array of activities from its luxurious five-star hotels, championship golf course, marina and recreational facilities, with future development of premier condominiums and bungalows. The elegant business setting of the Pacific Sutera Hotel is complemented by the resort ambience of the Magellan Sutera Hotel, offering a total of 956 guest rooms and suites of luxurious comfort.

–Sutera Harbour Resort, www.suteraharbour.com

SHANGRI-LA'S TANJUNG ARU RESORT
SHANGRI-LA'S RASA RIA RESORT

Shangri-La's Tanjung Aru Resort
Locked Bag 174, 88995 Kota Kinabalu
Sabah, Malaysia
Tel: 6088.225.800, Fax: 6088.217.155
Email: tah@shangri-la.com
http://www.shangri-la.com

Shangri-La's Rasa Ria Resort
Pantai Dalit Beach,
P.O. Box 600, 89208 Tuaran
Sabah, East Malaysia
Tel: 6088.792.888, Fax: 6088.792.777
Email: rrr@shangri-la.com
http://www.shangri-la.com

The name Shangri-La was inspired by James Hilton's legendary novel, *Lost Horizon*. A tranquil haven in the mountains of Tibet, Shangri-La cast a spell on all who resided there. Today, Shangri-La stands as a synonym for Paradise. Although literary in origin, the name describes perfectly the genuine serenity and service for which Shangri-La Hotels and Resorts are known. Our vision: To be the dominant hotel company in Asia. Our mission: To be the dominant choice for our customers, employees, and shareholders. Our philosophy: Asian hospitality from caring people.

–Shangri-La Resorts, www.shangri-la.com

Common birdwing

Sambar deer

Contributor

Nexus Resort Karambunai

Nexus Resort Karambunai
Off Jalan Sapangar Bay
Kg. Karambunai, P. O. Box 270
88450 Menggatal
Sabah, Malaysia
Tel: 6088.411222
Fax: 6088.411020
Email: nexushtl@tm.net.my
http://www.borneo-resort.com

Nexus Resort Karambunai is set within 3,335 acres of unique and unspoiled beauty. It is the perfect getaway retreat for the discerning traveller, be it for vacations or business purposes. The resort is located 30 km northeast of Kota Kinabalu, the capital of Sabah, the eastern state of Malaysia, on the magnificent and majestic island of Borneo. If you plan to visit the Far East, you must not miss the romanticism and mysticism of Borneo, the last unexplored tropical paradise. While you are here, you will discover the true meaning of tranquillity, seclusion, and sheer luxury. Experience the many fascinations of Nexus Resort Karambunai, where nature, beauty, and luxury become one.

–Nexus Resort Karambunai, www.borneo-resort.com

Gorgonion coral

Leaf scorpionfish

Bumphead parrotfish

Long-nos

Supporters

Layang Layang Island Resort
Block A, Ground Floor, A-0-3, Megan Phileo Avenue
12 Jalan Yap Kwan Seng
50450 Kuala Lumpur, Malaysia
Tel: 603.262.2877
Fax: 603.262.2980
Email: layang@pop.jaring.my
http://www.layanglayang.com

Borneo Divers and Sea Sports
9th Floor, Menara Jubili,
53, Jalan Gaya,
88000 Kota Kinabalu
Sabah, Malaysia
Tel: 6088.222226
Fax: 6088.221550
Email: diving@bdiver.po.my
http://www.jaring.my/bdivers

Pulau Sipadan Resort and Tours
1st Floor, No. 484, Block P, Bandar Sabindo
P. O. Box 61120
91021 Tawau
Sabah, Malaysia
Tel: 6089.765200
Fax: 6089.763575
Email: psrt@po.jaring.my

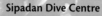

Sipadan Water Village Resort
TB 226, Lot 3, 1st Floor, Wisma MAA
Tawau
Sabah, Malaysia
Tel: 6089.752996
Fax: 6089.752997
Email: swv@sipadan-village.com.my
http://www.sipadan-village.com.my

Sipadan Dive Centre
A1103, 11th Floor, Wisma Merdeka, Jalan Tun Razak,
88000 Kota Kinabalu,
Sabah, Malaysia
Tel: 6088.240584
Fax: 6088.240415
Email: sipadan@po.jaring.my
http://www.sipadandivers.com

Reef scenic

Square spot anthia

List of Figures

Reefs and Rain Forests

The Natural Heritage of Malaysian Borneo

Book Designers	**❙**	Lea Eckerling Kaufman and Irina Averkieff
Editors	**❙**	Lea Eckerling Kaufman
		Nancy Lambert
		Irina Averkieff
Photo Editor	**❙**	Lea Eckerling Kaufman
Publishing Consultant	**❙**	Charles Mohr, LA Book Arts, Inc.
Typography	**❙**	Perpetua and Perpetua Expert
		Cronos , Waters Titling
		and Poetica Supplement Swash Caps IV
Text Paper	**❙**	150 GSM Nymolla Matt Art
Printing	**❙**	Tien Wah Press, Ltd., Singapore